BROTHERS IN ARMS

BROTHERS IN ARMS

The story of a British and a German
Fighter Unit, August to December 1940

Chris Goss

CRÉCY BOOKS

Published by Crécy Books Ltd, 1994
All rights reserved
© Christopher H Goss, 1994
ISBN 0 947554 37 8

Typeset in Baskerville by
Ace Filmsetting Ltd, Frome, Somerset

Printed and bound in Great Britain by
Hartnolls Limited, Bodmin, Cornwall

Contents

Acknowledgements

I have been lucky to have the support of many in writing this book, so many in fact, that if anyone is forgotten, I apologise profusely:

The RAF:

Sir Alec Atkinson DFC, Wg Cdt R P Beamont CBE, DSO & BAR, DFC & BAR, DL, Gp Capt John D Bisdee OBE, DFC, MA, Jim Earnshaw, the late Wg Cdr J R H Gayner DFC, Flt Lt S H 'Darkie' Hanson, the late Sqn Ldr J H Lacey DFM & BAR, Senator H de M Molson OBE, Sqn Ldr A K 'Keith' Ogilvie DFC, Wg Cdr P B Pitcher DFC, Sqn Ldr Jan Zurakowski DFC.

The Luftwaffe:

Siegfried Becker, Josef Bröker, Franz Fiby, Willi Ghesla, Max Guschewski, Heinrich Höhnisch, Werner Karl, Julius Meimberg, Wolf Münchmeyer, Hans Ohly, Walter Rupp, Ernst-Albrecht Schulz, Herbert Tzschoppe, Heinz-Eugen Wittmeyer, Heinz Zag, Alfred Zeis.

I would also like to thank the following; Winfried Bock, Peter Cornwell for giving me the ideas for this book, Graham Day for his considerable help over the years, Frau Hanne-Birgit Götz (daughter of the late Hans-Karl Mayer), Mark Postlethwaite, Bernd Rauchbach for his help and for arranging so much for me in Germany, Dilip Sarkar, Clive Williams for giving me the chance to put my research into print and Mrs Sonia Ziegler. Last but by no means least, I must acknowledge the support of my long-suffering wife Sally – I hope it has all been worth it!

Introduction

Many books have been written about the air war of the Second World War. Of these, much has been written about the Summer of 1940 and what later became known as the Battle of Britain. To date, no one has looked at elements of each of the opposing air forces and compared the two – what did each pilot think when pitted against another in a fight which, for many, was of life and death? What did each pilot think, be he German or British, when he had to climb again into the cramped, hot, fume-filled cockpit of his Messerschmitt Bf 109 or Spitfire and take off into the air on what could have been his last flight?

Some years ago, I received a letter from a former Luftwaffe fighter pilot. In his letter, he told me of how many flights he flew during the Summer of 1940; how many aircraft he shot down and what happened to him afterwards. The letter enclosed a few snaps for which he had no further use. One of the photos showed a group of nine smiling men, their arms linked. If one looked closely, very small Luftwaffe eagles could be seen on some of their tunics. These were the pilots of *1 Staffel/Jagdgeschwader 53* (literally 'First Squadron of the 53rd Fighter Group' – 1/JG 53 for short), the *Pik As* or 'Ace of Spades' *Geschwader*. I then took out a similar photo of another group of pilots – similar poses, similar smiles but no eagles on their tunics – only a Spitfire in the background indicated that these pilots were British and were in fact from Number 609 Squadron Royal Auxiliary Air Force whose motto, being from the West Riding of Yorkshire, was the apt hunting call of 'Tally Ho!'. Despite the undeniable fact that the former group of pilots were helping to further the aims of a dictator and his sick, misguided ideals and the latter group were the defenders of their nation, its people and freedom, there was little that one could see from these photos to differentiate the two groups of fighter pilots.

Eager to know more, I asked the former Luftwaffe pilot who was who in the photo – he identified all and from that, I was able to ascertain their fates. Of the nine in the photo, five were to be prisoners of war and one was to be killed in action within two months of that photo being taken. Of the remainder, one was to be reported missing early the following Summer, two were to survive the war one having been badly wounded more than once and the other having been shot down in action a number of times.

Looking at the group of RAF pilots made me wonder what happened to them, did they ever meet the above Germans in combat and what would they think of each other today – both countries now being closer together than ever before and fellow members of NATO and the European Economic Community? The results of my researches in to these two units are in the chapters of this book. This will hopefully show that despite Hitler and his aims and whatever else happened during the War, there was a sort of fighter pilot's affinity between these enemies to such an extent that today, they might possibly be regarded by some as 'brothers in arms'. This therefore is the story of 1/JG 53 and 609 Squadron – the combats fought, the sacrifices made and the thoughts of those men who survived.

Glossary

Bf	Bayerische Flugzeugwerke (Messerschmitt aircraft prefix)
Deckungsrotte	Lookout pair
Erprobungsgruppe (Erpr Gr)	Experimental Wing
Fähnrich (Fhr)	Officer cadet
Feldwebel (Fw)	Flight Sergeant (FS)
Flieger (Flg)	Aircraftsman
Fliegerkorps	Combat force made up of different *Geschwader*
Freie Jagd	Free hunting fighter sweep
Führer	Leader
Gefreiter (Gefr)	Leading aircraftsman
Geschwader	Group (three *Gruppen*); commanded by a *Geschwader Kommodore*
Gruppe	Wing (three *Staffeln*); commanded by a *Gruppen Kommandeur* (Gr Kdr)
Hauptmann (Hptm)	Flight Lieutenant (Flt Lt)
Jabo	Fighter bomber
Jagdgeschwader (JG)	Fighter Group
Kette	Three aircraft tactical formation
Kampfgeschwader (KG)	Bomber Group
Lehrgeschwader (LG)	Technical Development Flying Group
Leutnant (Lt)	Pilot Officer (Plt Off)
Luftflotte	Air Fleet
Major (Maj)	Squadron Leader (Sqn Ldr)
Oberfeldwebel (Ofw)	Warrant Officer (WO)
Obergefreiter (Ogefr)	Senior Aircraftsman
Oberleutnant (Oblt)	Flying Officer (Fg Off)
Oberst	Group Captain
Oberstleutnant (Obstlt)	Wing Commander
Pik As	Ace of Spaces
Rotte	Two aircraft tactical formation; two *Rotten* made a *Schwarm*; commanded by a *Rottenführer*
Rottenflieger	Wingman
Schwarm	Four aircraft tactical formation; commanded by a *Schwarm* leader
Sonderführer (Sd Fhr)	Rank usually given to war reporters
Stab	Staff or Headquarters (formation in which *Gruppenkommandeur* or *Geschwader Kommodore* usually flew)
Staffel	Squadron (twelve aircraft); commanded by a *Staffelkapitän* (St Kap)
Sturzkampfgeschwader (StG)	Dive bomber group – usually shortened to Stuka
Unteroffizier (Uffz)	Sergeant (Sgt)
Werk Nummer (Wk Nr)	Serial number
Zerstoerergeschwader (ZG)	Heavy fighter group

CHAPTER ONE

The Two Sides Meet

By Saturday 24th of August 1940, Great Britain had experienced a taste of things to come. The Luftwaffe, now rested since 19th of August because of the bad weather, was about to commence what contemporary historians now call *Phase Three* of the Battle of Britain – a phase which was intended to result in the destruction of Fighter Command's ability to counter any German invasion of Great Britain. *Phase One*, the Luftwaffe's attempt to achieve air superiority over the English Channel, had lasted from the 10th of July to the 7th of August 1940 whilst *Phase Two*, an all out attack on the RAF's fighter defence system, had lasted from the 8th to the 23rd of August 1940. With both phases, the Germans had not achieved their aims. Nevertheless, as a fine and clear dawn broke on the 24th, the Luftwaffe crews prepared to carry out the latest tactical order whilst RAF Fighter Command prepared itself for yet another series of German onslaughts.

The initial action on the 24th was restricted, in the first part of the day, to Fighter Command's 11 Group based in the south-east of England. However, at about 1540 hours, the radar station at Ventnor on the Isle of Wight, badly damaged in *Phase Two* attacks but now just about back on line, began to pick up a formation of one hundred plus aircraft north of the Somme Estuary and which appeared to be headed towards the Portsmouth and Southampton area. The Controllers in 10 Group put their Squadrons on readiness and prepared for the worst.

The formation picked up by Ventnor consisted of twenty-five Junkers Ju 88A bombers of *I Gruppe/Kampfgeschwader 51* (I/KG 51) and twenty-one Junkers Ju 88As of III/KG 51. Escort was provided by sixty-three Messerschmitt Bf 109E's of *I* and *II Gruppen/JG 53* (I and II/JG 53), sixty-nine Messerschmitt Bf 109Es of JG 2 and seventy-one Messerschmitt Bf 109Es of JG 27 as well as forty-four Messerschmitt Bf 110Cs of *Zerstörergeschwader 2* (ZG 2) and a further fifty-five Messerschmitt Bf 110s of *V (Zerstörer)/Lehrgeschwader 1* (V(Z)/LG 1). Amongst the 302 escorting German fighters, the pilots of I/JG 53 had been given the specific task of staying with the bombers, leaving the fighters of II/JG 53 to hopefully draw the RAF fighters away from the main formation. At about 1330 hours, following their briefing by their *Staffelkapitän, Hauptmann* Hans-Karl Mayer, pilots of 1/JG 53 climbed into their fighters, took off from their airfield at Rennes and headed towards their advance airfield of Cherbourg-East where the planes were refuelled. With their fighters now able to operate at maximum range, all pilots had a final briefing and then took off at 1550

Junkers Ju 88A of
Kampfgeschwader 51

1/JG 53 on their way to
England

hours. Forming up with the rest of their *Gruppe*, the other fighter *Geschwadern* and, eventually, the bombers of KG 51, 1/JG 53 then headed for their target – the repair workshops and dry docks of Portsmouth's naval dockyard.

Meanwhile, the pilots of 609 Squadron were on standby in their dispersal at Middle Wallop near Andover in Hampshire. The pilots were making the most of the day's good weather, especially as they had seen little action since claiming five enemy aircraft destroyed and three probably destroyed nine days before and the following days of inactivity had been cursed with poor weather conditions. However, at 1610 hours, thirteen Spitfires were scrambled and ordered to patrol in between Portsmouth and St Catherine's Point on the Isle of Wight at a height of 10,000 feet. One of those pilots, Pilot Officer David Crook, voiced the opinion of the whole Squadron by saying that although there were other squadrons patrolling at different heights, being at such a low altitude, in order to combat any dive bombers, was not a comforting feeling when there were enemy fighters above them.

Shortly after 609 Squadron's arrival, the Portsmouth anti-aircraft guns opened fire; the sight was impressive as the barrage was enhanced by guns of the warships lying in harbour. Looking 5,000 feet above them, the RAF pilots could see the German formation wheeling and then at 1620 hours saw the bombers starting to drop their deadly cargo; at that height, they could do nothing to intervene. As the pilots of 609 Squadron looked up, the pilots of 1/JG 53 must have been looking down at them and the other RAF fighters wheeling about.

609 Squadron at their dispersal, Middle Wallop

5,000 feet higher than the Spitfires of 609 Squadron, Hans-Karl Mayer led his Staffel away from the main formation in an attempt to catch any unwary RAF fighters. At 1640 hours, the twenty-nine year old German was looking to improve his current score of fifteen British and French aircraft destroyed. Spotting three Hurricanes, he dived his fighter towards them – the German opened fire on the leader whilst the other two quickly dived away and he watched his ammunition home in on the luckless Hurricane. Closing from 150 meters to a mere twenty meters, he saw strikes on the fuselage and in and around the cockpit. Having expended twenty rounds of 20mm ammunition and 140 rounds of 7.92mm ammunition, he broke off the engagement and, convinced that the pilot was dead, aw his sixteenth victim of the war dive away to the south of the Isle of Wight.

A section from 609 Sqn takes off from Middle Wallop

Although no Hurricane can be matched with Hans-Karl Mayer's claim, at the same time, Pilot Officer Andy Mamedorf, an American pilot who had joined 609 Squadron at the start of the month, was bounced by a German fighter. His Spitfire received severe damage when a 20mm shell entered the rear fuselage, went through his radio and almost penetrated the pilot's armour plating. Lucky to get away with a slightly bruised back, he nursed his aircraft back to Middle Wallop and landed success-fully, although the tail wheel collapsed after he touched down. Closer inspection of the airframe showed another 20mm shell had shredded half of the starboard elevator and the whole aircraft was peppered with

7.92mm bullet holes. It is conjecture whether it was *Hauptmann* Mayer who caused the damage as Pilot Officer Mamedorf never saw his assailant and assumed it was a Messerschmitt Bf 110. Nevertheless, the Spitfire was so badly damaged that it had to be written off.

At the same time as Pilot Officer Mamedorf was dicing with death, two other Spitfires of 609 Squadron were receiving damage at the hands of the Luftwaffe. Both pilots, Flight Lieutenant Frank Howell, 'A' Flight Commander, and Flying Officer 'Novo' Nowierski, returned to base with a few holes in their fighters but, after running repairs by 609 Squadron's hard-working and long-suffering groundcrew, both were soon back in the battle.

Hptm *Hans-Karl Mayer,* Staffelkapitän *of 1/JG 53*

Pilot Officer Andy, Mamedorf and his damaged Spitfire

Meanwhile, back at 20,000 feet, twelve Spitfires of 234 Squadron, also based at Middle Wallop, were in a better position to intercept. Flying as 'Number Two' in the last of four sections was Polish Pilot Officer Jan Zurakowski. As his Squadron closed on the German formation, he noticed below about thirty-five twin-engined German aircraft. Deciding to try and get them himself, he broke formation and carried out an attack on the rear of the enemy formation. On seeing no results and having broken formation without permission, he thought he had better get back before he was missed. In his eagerness to get back he paid the price for his gamble.

Hans-Karl Mayer spotted the lone Spitfire to the east of the Isle of Wight and led the whole Staffel after it. His first burst caused the Spitfire to break left and into the line of fire of the leader of the second *Schwarm* of four Messerschmitts. *Leutnant* Alfred Zeis did not hesitate in firing a total of fifty-six 20mm rounds and 128 machine gun rounds into the Spitfire. Pilot Officer Zurakowski heard a very loud bang and lost all control of the elevators and rudder and his Spitfire soon went into a flat spin. Alfred Zeis noted with satisfaction, as the Spitfire spiralled downwards to crash to the eastern corner of the Isle of Wight, his second confirmed kill. Meanwhile, Pilot Officer Zurakowski had managed to extricate himself from the cockpit but did not open his parachute as, on looking skywards, he saw to his horror his Spitfire cartwheeling above him. Getting closer to the ground, he had no alternative but to pull the ripcord. Shortly afterwards, his parachute opened and he landed safely, to his relief, his Spitfire dropped belly-downwards alongside him in the same field close to the village of Merstone.

Pilot Officer Jan Zurakowski of 234 Squadron

Hptm *Hans-Karl Mayer*
and Lt *Alfred Zeis,*
victors of the 24 August
1940 combats

Zurakowski's problems did not end there. A member of the Home Guard, as shocked as the Polish pilot as he had seen both a plane and a pilot land next to him, was convinced that the man at the end of his double-barrelled shotgun was German and, not speaking the 'Kings' English, the Pole only managed to convince the poor man even more. To add insult to injury, even after the Pole had handed him his RAF identity card, he was unable to read details as his hands were shaking so much! Eventually the situation sorted itself out with the arrival of an Army unit who posted a guard on the Spitfire. Their officer, having a steadier hand and therefore able to check the identity card, whisked the pilot away to their headquarters.

Back at 20,000 feet, the Germans had done what they intended to do and were heading back to the safety of France. In Portsmouth, 104 civilians lay dead and 237 injured in addition to more than fifty casualties to Royal

Navy personnel. According to British sources over 200 bombs had landed on both the Dockyard and, by accident, on the City itself in the space of less than four minutes; one fire caused by the raid continued to rage for a further day and a half. For the Luftwaffe the raid was a success as they had in fact dropped a total of 123 bombs of varying size in the space of three minutes and had succeeded in hitting the target and drawing up the defending fighters. However, it was noted that some of III/KG 51's bombs had landed on the city. The German fighters claimed a total of five aircraft destroyed as, in addition to the 1/JG 53 claims, *Leutnant* Wilhelm Heidemeier of 2/JG 53 claimed a Spitfire (although this was later disallowed) whilst JG 2 claimed the remainder with *Oberfeldwebel* Hans Klee of 7/JG 2 and *Unteroffizier* Werner of III/JG 2 both claiming a Spitfire each. The attackers lost four aircraft. A Junkers Ju 88A-1 of 7/KG 51 was so badly damaged by anti-aircraft fire that it ditched mid-Channel on the way back, resulting in the deaths of *Unteroffizier* Maurer and *Unteroffizier* Schultz and *Gefreiter* Pfaff (one crew member was rescued uninjured). The single seat fighter losses were two Messerschmitt Bf 109's of 6/JG 2, *Feldwebel* Gerhard Ebus drowning in the Solent (his aircraft crashing near Ventnor) and *Feldwebel* Otto Werner being rescued after ditching, the pilot suffering slight wounds. The final German loss was a Messerschmitt Bf 110C-4 of 5/ZG 2 which ditched thirty-five kilometres north of Cherbourg and although both crew members got out, the pilot, *Leutnant* Juergen Meyer, drowned whilst his wounded radio operator, *Feldwebel* Henry Schneider, was successfully rescued. RAF claims for these German fighters were filed by Squadron Leader Joseph O'Brien (Messerschmitt Bf 109 destroyed), Pilot Officer William Gordon (Messerschmitt Bf 109 destroyed), Pilot Officer Keith Lawrence (Messerschmitt Bf 110 damaged), Pilot Officer Zbigniew Olenski (Messerschmitt Bf 109 probably destroyed) and Flight Lieutenant Robert Barton (Messerschmitt Bf 109 destroyed). All of these RAF pilots, except Barton who was from 249 Squadron, came from 234 Squadron.

So finished the first air combat where 609 Squadron and 1/JG 53 were definitely involved together. 609 Squadron returned to base annoyed that 'no scalps were obtained', in the words of Flight Sergeant 'Tich' Cloves, one of 609 Squadron's ground crew and unofficial diarist, but were thankful that none of its pilots were killed or wounded. Landing at 1715 hours, the Squadron was stood down and had the opportunity to lick its wounds, all be they slight, and to wonder what the next day would bring. Back on the Isle of Wight, a relieved Pilot Officer Zurakowski must have been thanking the Gods. Although not from 609 Squadron, Zurakowski had definitely met 1/JG 53 (though, coincidentally, in a month and a half, he would find himself flying with 609 Squadron). Meanwhile, five minutes before 609 Squadron landed, a happy 1/JG 53 landed back at Cherbourg-East, no doubt wondering what the following day or next mission would bring. They were lucky this time but would they now be able to increase the Staffel score of forty-five kills since the start of the war and again not lose any pilots? In exactly twenty-three hours both sides would know.

CHAPTER TWO

Good Day Sir — How Are You?

During the night of the 24th–25th August 1940, the Luftwaffe carried out sporadic attacks on parts of south east England, with Headquarters Number 11 Group tasking a number of its day fighters to carry out 'cat's eyes' patrols along the south coast. To the west, the pilots of Number 10 Group had a much quieter night but as dawn broke on the Sunday, Fighter Command, seeing that the weather was similar to the previous day, expected a repeat performance and not a day of rest. Apart from Luftwaffe fighters flying up and down the Channel on *Freie Jagd* or 'free chase' missions, probably in the hope of either drawing up RAF fighters or just irritating the defenders, it was not until the late afternoon that radar screens picked up activity over France and as before, it appeared that the Luftwaffe was heading towards a target in the west of England – 10 Group and 609 Squadron's territory.

On the morning of the 25th of August, the pilots of 1/JG 53 had the opportunity to lie on in their billets. One of these pilots was twenty-two year old *Gefreiter* Josef Bröker. Josef had joined *1 Staffel* on the 14th of August 1940, excited at being a member of one of the 'Ace of Spades' Geschwader's more successful Staffeln. However, for the first week, he had to content himself with getting used to how the Staffel operated, not yet being allowed by his *Staffelkapitän* to fly operationally. This gave him time to photograph his new aircraft, coded 'white 15' and, more excitingly for him, to photograph something he expected to meet in the skies over England – a Spitfire of 234 Squadron which landed at the airfield of Cherbourg-East in the afternoon of the 15th of August. *Hauptmann* Mayer did feel confident to use him as his wingman on the 24th of August mission when Josef stuck to him like glue during the combats fought.

Nevertheless, all of the Staffel must have hoped that there were to be no missions flown this day so that they could catch up with letter writing or go to a restaurant in Rennes for their usual lobster and oysters.

Their day of rest was not to be as at some point during the morning, the Staffel drove to their dispersal and the three *Staffelkapitäne* of I/JG 53, *Hauptmann* Mayer, *Oberleutnant* Ignatz Prestelle of 2/JG 53 and *Hauptmann* Wolfgang Lippert of 3/JG 53, were summoned by their *Gruppenkommandeur*, *Major* Albert Blumensaat, for a mission brief. The remainder of *1 Staffel* waited nervously for *Hauptmann* Mayer's return and when he did, he called all together to tell them that again they were escorting Junkers Ju 88s who this time would attack the airfield of Warmwell in Dorset. Hans-

Gefreiter *Josef Bröker*,
1/*JG 53, August 1940*

*Briefing for the I/JG 53
pilots at Rennes. Left to
right: ?,* Hauptmann
*Pingel (*StKap 2/*JG
53),* Hauptmann
*Mayer (*StKap 1/*JG
53),* Oberleutnant
Dittmar, Major
*Blumensaat (*GrKdr *I/
JG 53), ?,* Lt *Schultz, ?,*
Oblt *Ohly*

Karl Mayer decided that Josef Bröker would fly as the reserve pilot and would take his Messerschmitt with them to Cherbourg-East in case one of the Staffel failed to take off.

At 1110 hours the Staffel took off from Rennes on the forty minute flight to Cherbourg-East. They were scheduled to take off later that afternoon so all had a few hours to kill, most lazing around their tent or checking their fighters. Josef decided to visit the small German-run shop on the airfield but could not see anything that took his fancy. As he turned to leave, he was asked if he wanted a box of matches; all pilots smoked, he was told. Josef, being a non-smoker, declined but the salesman threw him the box saying that 'you never knew when matches would come in useful'. He put them into a pocket in his flying suit and headed back to dispersal.

Oblt *Ignatz Prestelle,*
StKap *2/JG 53*

Opposite above
Oblt *Lippert*, StKap *of
3/JG 53 (far right) with,
left to right* Oblt
Prestelle, Lt *Leonhard
and* Hptm *Pingel*

Opposite below
*1/JG 53's tent at
Cherbourg-East*

Close to 1630 hours, Hans-Karl Mayer called his Staffel together and gave them the final briefing. He confirmed who would be in which *schwarm* or *rotte* , who would be the *Holzaugenrotte* or 'lookout pair' and what tactics they would follow it attacked. Finally, he confirmed take-off time and at what time they were to meet up over Cherbourg. All of them then synchronised their watches. With his usual 'We're off! All the best!', the *Staffelkapitän* strode off towards his fighter followed by his Staffel. All over the airfield mechanics were running about and the sound of Daimler Benz engines began to increase in volume. Eighty-one fighters from JG 53 waited for the order to taxi, usually signalled by a flare, throttles were then opened and in order, all proceeded to the take-off position, opened throttles to full and, unsteadily at first, took to the air. At 1650 hours, 1/JG 53 became airborne. Tucked in behind the *Staffelkapitän* was a very excited Josef Bröker, one of the Staffel had problems on start up so he had taken that pilot's place. He was greatly reassured to have the protection of his *Staffelkapitän* and the two more experienced pilots in the *rotte* flying behind him.

In between 1520 and 1529 hours, nine heavily laden Junkers Ju 88As of I/KG 51, sixteen from II/KG 51 and twelve from III/KG 51 had taken off from their respective airfields of Melun-Villaroche, Orly and Etampes-Mondesir and headed towards Cherbourg. Off Cherbourg the bombers met up with their escorts and all set course for Warmwell. In addition to the Messerschmitt Bf 109s of JG 53, escort was also provided by fifty-nine Messerschmitt Bf 109s of JG 2 and a further seventy-four from JG 27

*One of the KG 51 pilots
who took part in the raid
was* Uffz *Robert Ciuraj
of 4/KG 51*

as well as a Messerschmitt Bf 110 escort made up of forty-six aircraft from I & II/ZG 2, thirty-seven from III/ZG 76 and twenty from *V/Lehrgeschwader 1* (V/LG 1). It must have been at this stage that the 354 aircraft formation's intention and route became clear to Fighter Command.

At Middle Wallop, 609 Squadron also had the pleasure of a quiet morning, even if on readiness. Sitting in and around the house that was their Headquarters, the pilots relaxed, chatting and playing cards. After lunch, they continued killing time, probably feeling tired of waiting for something to happen. As tea time neared, the warning of the approaching formation was passed and at 1700 hours, fourteen Spitfires of 609 Squadron were scrambled to patrol Swanage. This time they were not patrolling below the Germans so, as the enemy formation came into view, 609 Squadron and the other squadrons from Number 10 Group together with eleven Hurricanes of 17 Squadron from Tangmere and nine Spitfires of 602 Squadron from Westhampnett (both 11 Group airfields), were in an ideal position to attack.

As the formation approached Portland, 1/JG 53 broke away west below the bombers and above the other *Pik As* fighters and started to fly in between Portland and Weymouth looking for RAF victims. At 1723 hours the first bomber had reached Warmwell and despite the attentions of the

609 Squadron's HQ at Middle Wallop

Hurricane of 87 Squadron RAF, dropped its load then headed back south. 1/JG 53 then spotted a Hurricane squadron approaching from the north west, almost definitely 87 Squadron based at Exeter, but despite turning in behind the Hurricanes, they could do nothing to prevent the RAF pilots from wading in to the Messerschmitt Bf 110's on their way towards the bombers.

Meanwhile 609 Squadron had met the Messerschmitt Bf 110's of I/ZG 2 over Wareham and started to inflict punishment on the panicked formation. *Unteroffizier* Siegfried Becker, a pilot in 1/ZG 2, heard his radio operator *Obergefreiter* Walter Wötzel scream 'Break left!' and open fire as Pilot Officers Geoffrey Gaunt and Noel Agazarian of 609 Squadron dived on him. Geoffrey Gaunt, on his first operational flight, turned inside the diving German fighter firing short bursts as did Noel Agazarian. Gaunt fired until all his ammunition was exhausted and at 3,000 feet both RAF pilots lost sight of the Messerschmitt. All alone, Becker hoped to make it back to at least the mid-way point in the Channel in the hope that if he and Walter Wötzel baled out, they would be picked up by the German Air Sea Rescue. However, at 1,000 feet with the port engine on fire and the starboard engine streaming coolant and seizing, Becker threw off the cabin roof and ordered his gunner to bale out, following him shortly afterwards. Meanwhile Pilot Officers Gaunt and Agazarian descended to 500 feet and spotted the German fighter break through a thin layer of cloud on its back and hit the ground twenty yards from the River Frome at East Holme near Wareham. The German crew landed, one each side of a railway cutting in the field next to where their plane had crashed, Walter Wötzel breaking his foot in landing awkwardly. Shortly afterwards they were captured by British soldiers and taken to Portland.

It was about this time that the Messerschmitt Bf 109s intervened but not before the defending fighters had broken up the bomber formation. According to records, only seven bombers got through dropping twenty bombs which damaged two hangars, sick quarters and disrupted the telephone lines. Hans-Karl Mayer saw Hurricanes attacking the Junkers Ju 88's and shouted 'Everyone attack!', as he opened fire at a Hurricane from fifty metres, closing to ten metres. Firing eighteen rounds of 20mm ammunition and one hundred rounds of 7.92mm ammunition, the Hurricane burst into flames and at 1,000 feet, the pilot baled out, landing in the sea to the west of Portland, 500 yards off the coast. This Hurricane was possibly the one flown by Flight Lieutenant Alfred Bayne of 17 Squadron who was shot down and baled out uninjured off Portland at about 1725 hours. Following this, the combat became a wheeling mass of fighters and fleeing bombers.

Having dived through the escorting Messerschmitt Bf 110s, 609 Squadron joined in the mêlée. Sergeant Alan Feary watched with satisfaction as the *Staffelkapitän* of 1/ZG 1, *Oberleutnant* Gerhard Götz, and his gunner *Unteroffizier* Kurt Haupt, baled out of their crippled fighter which crashed just outside Wareham. Flight Lieutenant James 'Butch' McArthur, 'B' Flight Commander, Pilot Officer Eugene 'Red' Tobin, another American pilot flying with the RAF, and Flight Lieutenant Frank Howell each claimed a Messerschmitt Bf 110 destroyed whilst Squadron Leader Horace Darley and Pilot Officer Johnny Curchin each claimed a Messerschmitt Bf 109 destroyed off the coast. Two RAF pilots were on the

Messerschmitt Bf 110 of 1/ZG 2

receiving end. Pilot Officer David Crook forgot to throttle back diving on a Messerschmitt Bf 110 and in breaking away to avoid collision, presented the German gunner with a good target. The German fired a short burst which put several bullets through the wing very close to the fuselage and even closer to David Crook's leg! However, the second pilot was luckier, Pilot Officer Piotr 'Osti' Ostazewski had a 20mm shell blow off his top rear armour plating which then hit him on the head whilst another went through the top of his engine and out through the airscrew. A third shell severed the brake pipes so on landing he was unable to slow down sufficiently to prevent himself running through a hedge. However, in both cases, the Spitfires were repairable.

At the same time, the battle between 1/JG 53 and the Hurricanes continued. In the space of six minutes the Staffel had claimed a further six Hurricanes but in the confusion, Hans-Karl Mayer heard his *Rottenflieger* shout 'I've been hit!' again and again until he answered, telling him to land in England or bale out. After that there was silence.

Josef Bröker had felt his fighter shake violently, then climb, stall, roll over and go into a spin without warning. Behind him was Pilot Officer Walter Beaumont flying a Spitfire from 152 Squadron based at Warmwell who managed to get in a burst and saw the Messerschmitt stall. He followed the German fighter downwards and on the third burst saw glycol stream from its engine. Sergeant Reg Llewellyn of 213 Squadron also reported carrying out a stern attack on the same aircraft as did Pilot Officer Roland Beamont of 87 Squadron.

Josef Bröker's 'White 15' shortly before its demise

Flying Officer Roland Beamont, 87 Squadron

Meanwhile, oblivious of the RAF fighters lining up behind him, Josef Bröker was fighting to regain control of his fighter. Round and round the fighter spun, its pilot seeing green fields one moment, the Channel next. Still he could not regain control of the Messerschmitt. It was then that he called on the radio that he was hit and heard the reassuring voice of his *Staffelkapitän*. Still spinning, he saw two burning fighters, whether German or British he did not know or care, plunge past and he prepared himself to die. On closing his eyes the image of his mother flashed into his brain, crying at the death of her son and with a start, he opened his eyes, felt his plane shudder and feeling some pressure on his control column he managed, at about 3,000 feet, to recover from the spin. By now his engine had seized, the airscrew windmilling in the airstream. Looking about him he could see three or four RAF fighters. Escape being impossible as he was now at 500 feet, he looked for a field in which to land. Walter Beaumont sat watching this fight for life, noting two Hurricanes firing at the Messerschmitt after he did. Eventually two miles north of Weymouth, near the village of Buckland Ripers, Josef Bröker calmly lowered his fighter onto the ground, finally slithering to a stop close to Tatton House Farm at 1730 hours.

Seeing the German crash-land, Walter Beaumont flew back towards the action; he was to visit the site of the crash later that evening. Josef Bröker opened the cockpit roof to see the Hurricane of Roland Beamont fly over at about fifty feet and head off back towards Exeter. Calmly, the German took off his scarf, soaked it with fuel from the fuel primer pump in the cockpit and, remembering the matches he had been given back in Cherbourg took one out, struck it and put it to his scarf. He then threw his scarf into the fuel tank with dramatic results. His fighter exploded and he staggered away from the conflagration with burns to his hands and face. All of this was witnessed by a pilot of 609 Squadron. David Crook, who was looking for more 'trade', had just seen a Messerschmitt Bf 109 dive vertically into the sea off Chesil Bank (probably *Hauptmann* Alois Maculan of 6/JG 53 and a victim of either 609's Squadron Commander or Flying Officer Kenneth Tait of 87 Squadron) when he saw a Messerschmitt 109 with its engine stopped and followed by a Spitfire, glide down to make a forced landing near the coast. He then watched the pilot get out and set fire to the machine.

When Josef Bröker regained consciousness, lying on his back close to the burning plane, he saw two men standing over him, one of them saying 'Good day Sir, how are you?'. They took him to a farm house, bandaging his burns as best they could. Shortly after, soldiers arrived and after confirming that the burning Messerschmitt was his, drove him to Warmwell and the start of six and a half years of captivity.

For both 609 Squadron and 1/JG 53, the day had been a success. Landing back at Cherbourg at 1810 hours, the Germans were jubilant at getting seven more kills but they were sad to lose their newest member and only hoped that he was alive. On the 27th of August, Hans-Karl Mayer wrote to Josef's father with the sad news that his son had failed to return from an operational sortie to England. His letter continued:

Apparently taken by Lt
*Schultz during the 25
August 1940 combat a
damaged Hurricane tries
to evade its attacker*

*A 609 Spitfire is re-
armed after combat,
Middle Wallop*

. . . I ask you to let us know if you get any information via the Red Cross, as far as I am concerned, I will not fail to send you any information as well. It was your son's second mission to England and despite the short time he belonged to the Staffel, he fitted in well and was a good comrade.

With German Greetings

Hans Mayer

609 Squadron were much happier, the entry in their Operational Record Book being in a much lighter vein than the previous day, even making special comment about Pilot Officer Tobin's misfortune at blacking out in combat! Yet again, both unit's paths had crossed being involved in the same combat with similar experiences (and again, coincidentally, Pilot Officer Roland Beamont was later to join and command 609 Squadron).

Having seen the connection between the two sides, despite the difference in politics, aims and ideals between them, their thoughts and fears both before, during and after they put their lives on the line each day during the months August–December 1940 must have been similar. Surely, fear, trepidation, sadness and joy must have been the same mix of emotions irrespective of nationality? What then were the British, Canadian, Polish and American pilots of 609 Squadron and the German and Austrian pilots of 1/JG 53 really like and can comparisons be drawn?

Full details of Luftwaffe and RAF kills and losses for the 25th of August combat can be found in the appendices – *Author*

CHAPTER THREE

Prelude to the Battle (1)

609 Squadron, Royal Auxiliary Air Force was formed at Yeadon (now Leeds Bradford) airport on the 10th of February 1936 as ordered by Air Ministry Order Number 6/1936. This order was an attempt by the Air Ministry to match the expanding regular Air Force, expanding because of the rise of Hitler and the threat from the new German Air Force, with a corresponding increase in auxiliary squadrons. Formed initially as a bomber squadron it changed to a fighter squadron in December 1938. Over the months and years that followed, many local men from all walks of life joined 609 Squadron as aircrew and groundcrew. All were unaware that within three and a half years of their Squadron's birth, their country would be at War with Germany and in four and a half years, some of them would be fighting for their lives in a Squadron which was destined to be part of Fighter Commands front line in the Battle of Britain.

When on the 27th of August 1939 the Squadron proceeded to its war station, ten of its twenty-four pilots would be destined to fight in some part of the Battle of Britain. Of these twenty-four, only five would still be flying with the Squadron during the period covered by this book. These pilots were Flying Officer Stephen Beaumont who was a solicitor in civilian life, Flying Officer Alexander Edge (known as 'Paul' or 'Grandpa' because of his age) who was a technical representative with I G Dyestuffs of Bradford, Pilot Officer John Dundas (known as 'Scruffy' or 'Dogs') who was a journalist with *The Yorkshire Evening Post*, Pilot Officer David Crook who worked for a sports equipment company, Pilot Officer Michael Appleby and Pupil Pilot Geoffrey Gaunt who was a manufacturers assistant. The last three Squadron members were not fully trained as fighter pilots and when war was declared soon found themselves undergoing intensive flying training before rejoining their Squadron in 1940.

When Prime Minister Neville Chamberlain made his historic speech announcing that Britain was at war with Germany, 609 Squadron was at Catterick in North Yorkshire where it was being re-equipped with the new Supermarine Spitfire Is which were arriving in twos and threes to replace its aged Hawker Hind biplanes. Having completed the change to Spitfires, in October 1939 the Squadron headed north to Drem in East Lothian, via Acklington in Northumberland, where it was destined to sit out the 'Phoney War'. Although away from any action in the south of the country, the Squadron had to be content spending its time with convoy patrols and the occasional scramble as well as honing its skills with their new fighters. All

*Hawker Hinds of 609
Squadron*

*609 groundcrew pose with
their new fighter – a
Spitfire Mark I*

One of three early accidents – Flying Officer Proudmans's Spitfire burns after an accident on 15 May 1940

Even more groundcrew admire Sergeant Beard's spectacular accident, 26 February 1940

hoped that these skills would stand them in good stead if and when the Luftwaffe launched itself against them *en masse*.

As 1939 came to a close, the Squadron was still waiting to receive its baptism of fire. Nevertheless, it was lucky not to have lost any of its pilots either in action or accidents (although some Spitfires had been lost in various inevitable accidents). However, on the 29th of January 1940, three pilots from Red Section of 'A' Flight managed to damage a Heinkel He 111 of *Kampfgeschwader 26* (KG 26) and the Squadron's score card was almost open. Red must have been the lucky colour as two days short of a month later, Red Section which was patrolling off Saint Abbs Head, spotted a Heinkel He 111 of the same German unit and after a short combat, shot it down. One Spitfire was damaged receiving fourteen repairable bullet holes but this could not dampen 609 Squadron's joy at finally having a crack at the enemy.

609's groundcrew admire Flying Officer Dundas' handiwork, 28 March 1940

A Heinkel He 111 of Kampfgeschwader 26 *after meeting the RAF on 9 February 1940*

In the months that followed, the Luftwaffe failed to lock horns with 609 Squadron again over Scottish skies. As the Squadron Adjutant wrote in the Operations Record Book for April 1940:

> April has been an extremely quiet month from the point of view of Operational Flying. Every opportunity has been taken to get the maximum amount of practice flying – particularly flight attacks on flights and sections of Blenheim fighters . . .

Ten days into May, Germany invaded the Low Countries. Eight days after the invasion of the Low Countries, 609 Squadron was ordered to move to the airfield at Northolt on the outskirts of London. With fear and trepidation, the Squadron packed up and headed south.

Northolt was, at the time of 609 Squadron's arrival, home to a number of Squadrons – 92 Squadron equipped with Spitfires, 600 Squadron with Bristol Blenheim fighters, 111 and 85 Squadrons with Hawker Hurricanes. With the rapidly changing front line, many other Squadrons came under Northolt's command. For example, 253 Squadron with Hurricanes began operating with 111 Squadron for experience. It was this confused and busy station that greeted the pilots and groundcrew of 609 Squadron.

The relatively 'green' West Riding Squadron pilots soon realised what lay ahead for them. Eager not to fail in their first combat, they sought out any pilot who had experience with the Luftwaffe and tried to get as much information as possible on Luftwaffe tactics and aircraft. Meanwhile, the

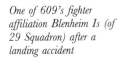

One of 609's fighter affiliation Blenheim Is (of 29 Squadron) after a landing accident

609 Squadron in their new dispersal, Northolt, 24 May 1940

One of 609's groundcrew, Johnny Payne, takes a break from working on his Spitfire

groundcrews were busy getting their Spitfires ready for combat which included adding extra armour plating to the back of the pilot's seat. The last batch of spares, including the armour plating, arrived on the 29th of May and on the 30th, within hours of the modification's completion, at 1215 hours twelve Spitfires of 609 Squadron took to the air and set course for the skies over Dunkirk to cover the British Expeditionary Force's evacuation.

The patrol area over Dunkirk was being bombed incessantly by the Luftwaffe but for 609 Squadron, the weather was so bad that they did not see any sign of the enemy and no contact was made. Slightly dejected, the Squadron headed back to Northolt. Unfortunately, bad luck struck as even worse weather was encountered over England causing Flying Officer Desmond Ayre to become lost; out of fuel, he killed himself attempting to force land his Spitfire. Three other pilots became lost but landed without injury to themselves.

From that day on, the Squadron began to take shape as a fighting machine. On the 31st of May it claimed two Messerschmitt Bf 109s destroyed, three Heinkel He 111s destroyed and two of the same type damaged, one Dornier Do 17 destroyed and a half share in a Junkers Ju 88 probably destroyed. Sadly, the Squadron suffered two pilots missing and another seriously wounded. The month of June 1940, from the view of combat with the enemy, only lasted one day. On the first, they shot down a Messerschmitt Bf 110 and damaged two Heinkel He 111s but lost two pilots missing believed killed in the process.

609's Spitfires ready for action at Northolt

*Taking a break before the
next mission, 1 June
1940. In the centre is
Flying Officer Frank
Howell who on this day
damaged a Heinkel He
111 off Dunkirk*

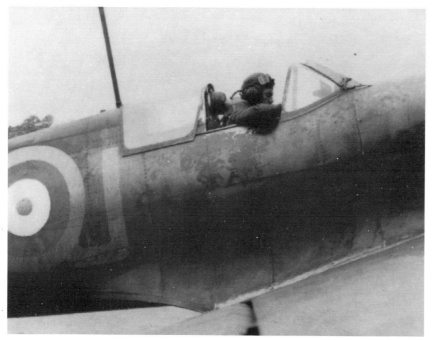

*1 June 1940 – Flying
Officer I B N Russell
takes off never to return.
Russell was awarded the
DFC posthumously*

Pilots and groundcrew relax in the Summer sunshine, Northolt, 3 June 1940

As the month of June 1940 continued, the Squadron buried its dead, carried out a few patrols without meeting any opposition; escorted Winston Churchill, Anthony Eden and Sir John Dill to and from a conference in France on two occasions and took advantage of the good weather by sunbathing and swimming. It was during this period that the Squadron's first award was gazetted when on the 13th of June a posthumous Distinguished Flying Cross (DFC) was awarded to Flying Officer I B N Russell who went missing on the first of the month. Its baptism of fire over, the Squadron continued to practice flying, tactics and gunnery for the inevitable German aerial onslaught. As the month came to a close, they and Britain were still waiting.

The next part of 609 Squadron's war was destined not to be fought from Northolt as on the 4th of July they were instructed to fly to Warmwell in Dorset and after that, to fly to Middle Wallop in Hampshire. Following a further two days of counter and counter-counter orders and total confusion, the Squadron was eventually declared operational finding itself being based at Middle Wallop with one flight to be based at Warmwell on rotation.

Soon the Luftwaffe made its presence felt with the Squadron's first scramble on the 7th of July, the first kill on the 9th of July and the next death, that of Flying Officer 'Pip' Drummond-Hay, also on the 9th. As July rolled into August, 609 Squadron had seen much action and for them the Battle of Britain had truly begun. However, the combats of July 1940 were mere skirmishes compared to what the rest of 1940 was about to bring.

CHAPTER FOUR

Bags of Joy, Sir?

By the beginning of August 1940, 609 were working to a settled operational programme with 238 and 152 Squadrons – 609 and 238 Squadrons being based at Middle Wallop, 152 Squadron at Warmwell. The routine went as follows:

> A day on fifteen minutes availability at Wallop; a day of release off camp; a day of readiness at Warmwell where we kept a servicing party of thirty airmen under Flight Sergeant Agar and Sergeant Fitzgerald.

So starts the entries in 609 Squadron's Operations Record Book (Form 540) for the month of August 1940 written by one of its pilots, Flying Officer John Dundas, chosen or volunteered because of his journalistic abilities. The air war over 609 Squadron's 'patch' had been quiet since the 27th of July when Pilot Officer James 'Buck' Buchanan had been shot down by *Oberleutnant* Gert Framm, *Staffelkapitän* of 2/JG 27 whilst on patrol over Weymouth Bay. With time on his hands, 609's diarist decided to start the next month's entries by setting the scene. As the month progressed, the entries were to become far less verbose.

As August commenced, a number of pilots found themselves either posted in or out of the Squadron. One of the saddest postings out was that of the 'old hand' Flight Lieutenant Stephen Beaumont, Officer Commanding 'B' Flight. On the 31st of July, he flew for the last time and, having admitted that he was getting a bit too old at thirty for flying fighters, was posted to 7 Operational Training Unit (OTU) at Hawarden on the 2nd of August. Also to go was Pilot Officer Jarvis Blayney. On the 29th of July he had blacked out whilst flying at 12,000 feet and only managed to come around when his Spitfire was at 1,000 feet and had to force-land his fighter at Boscombe Down. Because of that, the Medical Officer was forced to ban him from operational flying and he was posted to 6 Ferry Pool on the 16th of August. The final departure was Flying Officer Bernard Little. On the 2nd of August he was taken ill with appendicitis and on recovering from his operation, was posted to 9 Flying Training School. Happily, all three were to survive the war. Only five pre-war auxiliaries now remained – Flying Officers 'Grandpa' Edge, John Dundas and 'Mac' Goodwin* and Pilot Officers Michael Appleby and David Crook. For some, their fortunes as the battle and the war progressed were to be different.

---

* Goodwin had flown with 605 Squadron Royal Auxiliary Air Force before the war – *Author*

Flying Officer John
Dundas (far left)

Flight Lieutenant S G
Beaumont shortly before
leaving the Squadron

Replacements arrived almost immediately. Stephen Beaumont's position as 'B' Flight commander was taken by Flight Lieutenant James 'Butch' McArthur, an experienced pre-War regular pilot transferred from 238 Squadron on the other side of the airfield at Middle Wallop. The next were Polish – Flying Officers Tadeusz Nowierski and Piotr Ostazewski-Ostoja – 'Neither (of whom) could speak much English at the time but both rapidly acquired efficiency on Spitfires' reported John Dundas. Both were experienced pilots, Nowierski was aged thirty-one and Ostazewski thirty* and were pre-war regular members of the Polish Air Force. If they had difficulties with the English language, 609's Yorkshire pilots certainly must have had difficulty with their Polish names as they quickly became known as 'Novi' and 'Osti' respectively. Unusually, the next three replacements were also 'foreigners', Pilot Officers Andrew Mamedorf, Eugene 'Red' Tobin and Vernon 'Shorty' Keough came from the United States. Mamedorf and Tobin had signed up to fight in the Russia–Finland 'Winter' War but by the time they had arrived, it had finished. All of them had then made abortive attempts to join the French Air Force but eventually joined the RAF after the French surrender. After an intensive flying course lasting four weeks, they arrived from 7 OTU on the 6th of August.

*Note the comment made about Stephen Beaumont who was regarded as too old at thirty! – Author

609 get used to operating at Middle Wallop – getting to dispersal along the main Andover–Salisbury road

609 was now quite an international Squadron and the new pilots settled in quickly. The Commanding Officer, Squadron Leader Horace Darley, was aware of the Pole's eagerness for a fight but because of their lack of radio discipline (which must have been compounded by their poor English) he warned them that if he caught them speaking Polish in the air, he would ground them; their English improved dramatically and he never carried out his threat. The Americans were different altogether, Tobin was casual in both outlook and manner, Mamedorf had a penchant for gambling and Keough, being a mere four feet ten inches tall, needed cushions to see out of the windscreen of his Spitfire. Even their peace time jobs matched their personalities as Tobin had worked at the Metro Goldwyn Mayer Studios in California, Mamedorf had been a flying instructor and barnstormer whilst Keough was a professional parachute jumper (some of 609's pilots believing this to be the reason why 'Shorty' was so short!). However, all must have been keen to fly and fight and Squadron Leader Darley was aware of this, making sure that they were trained to his satisfaction before he would allow them to fly operationally.

Nevertheless, the influx of new pilots was welcomed by the existing Squadron members. David Crook wrote in his classic book *Spitfire Pilot** that:

> The influx of new blood played a big part in bringing an end to our run of bad luck, because from now onwards, we started on an almost unbroken series of successes and victories.

* First published by *Faber & Faber*, 1942

As far as 609 Squadron was aware, the Battle of Britain and this 'unbroken series of successes and victories' was to begin on Thursday 8th of August 1940.

Phase Two of the Luftwaffe's aerial assault against the United Kingdom commenced on the 8th of August and the focus of German attention was against Convoy CW 9 code named PEEWIT. Attempting to transit the Channel from east to west, twenty plus merchant ships with their Royal Navy escort had left the River Medway estuary under the cover of darkness on the night of the 7th of August but soon were detected by the Germans whilst sailing through the Straits of Dover. Attacks by German E-Boats soon followed, sinking three ships, and as dawn broke over the Channel, it was the Luftwaffe's turn to attack the hapless convoy.

609 Squadron flew at least three separate patrols on this day. The first a patrol over Swanage against a raid of thirty plus at about 0900 hours was uneventful. However, at 1130 hours, 'B' Flight was scrambled to patrol PEEWIT, 'A' Flight scrambling twenty-five minutes later. The five Spitfires of 'B' Flight located the convoy about twelve miles south of Bournemouth but whilst flying in a thin layer of cloud, became separated. As they reformed, Pilot Officer David Crook spotted balloons falling in flames over the convoy and noticed aircraft circling the ships. Tightening their harnesses and checking their firing buttons were on 'fire', 609 flew full throttle towards the enemy.

PEEWIT was under attack by Junkers Ju 87 Stukas from *Luftflotte 3* protected by a heavy escort of Messerschmitt Bf 110s and Messerschmitt Bf 109's. By the time 609 reached the convoy, all the balloons had been

The Junkers Ju 87 (seen here from 1/StG 1)

John Curchin climbs into his Spitfire

shot down and a number of ships were on fire or sinking; as 609 Squadron and the other RAF fighter squadrons waded in, the sky became full of vicious dogfights. Squadron Leader Darley managed to shoot down a Messerschmitt Bf 110 and then put his 'Number Two', Pilot Officer Michael Appleby in such a position for an attack on a Messerschmitt Bf 110 that:

> All I had to do was press the firing button and both the engine cowlings and cockpit came off and the aircraft was seen to dive into the sea, much to the delight, we subsequently heard, of the Royal Navy.

David Crook, who was Number Two to his Flight Commander might have had similar luck if he had not got separated as 'Butch' McArthur managed to shoot down two of the Stukas on their way back to France. The final kill, another 110, was claimed by Australian-born Pilot Officer Johnny Curchin who had joined the Squadron back in June 1940 as a replacement for one of the pilots lost over Dunkirk. It was not only Curchin's but all of the successful pilots' first kills of the war and, out of ammunition and replaced by 'A' Flight, all flew back to Middle Wallop exhilarated and happy that the only casualties of the action were two Spitfires with a few repairable bullet holes.*

The Squadron's morale took a sudden leap for the better and John Dundas was able to write in the Squadron's Operations Record Book:

> Four pilots engaged and accounted for five Huns. Though a good day for
> 609 Squadron, this was a bad day for the Navy.

However, David Crook was very annoyed at being the only pilot of the engagement not to make a claim. He was also concerned at the apparent change that had come over his Flight Commander whose first operational flight with 609 had resulted in 'two kills'; Crook saw him becoming over-confident. On a later patrol that day, 'Butch' took them too close to Cherbourg for comfort but without any dire consequences. Such over confidence could be a fatal thing and it was hoped that it would not have disastrous results in the next big combat. Crook's concern was to be unfounded when three days later 609 went into action again.

Two days of inactivity followed, with only the occasional uneventful patrol. The only flight worth noting was that of Pilot Officer 'Red' Robin who was detailed on the 9th of August to fly his Commanding Officer's Spitfire, one of the two damaged in the 8th of August combat, to Hamble near Southampton for repairs to bullet holes. Quickly repaired, the Spitfire was ready the next day but on take off, Tobin pushed the stick too far forward and hit the ground with the tips of the propeller blades. The result was the Spitfire had to remain at Hamble and the unfortunate pilot had to return by road to tell his Commanding Officer what he had done to his personal Spitfire. The only comments recorded were that Squadron Leader Darley wrote 'Blast it!' on the serviceability board and presumably vented his annoyance on Tobin when he returned.

It was about now that 609 Squadron began to find the facilities at Warmwell somewhat lacking. The day's detachment was described as always being 'one of action and discomfort.' John Dundas complained in the Operations Record Book about the sleeping accommodation, unreli-able telephones, the dust and stones always thrown up whenever a fighter started up and the lack of things to entertain pilots whilst waiting at dispersal. However, the main criticism concerned the meals and was graphically illustrated by Dundas's comments:

> . . . there were not many of these and the whole question of meals became
> a bone of contention between the Station authorities and the Squadron. It
> was impossible for pilots to turn up at the Mess for meals at any fixed time
> since operations would only relax readiness as and when circumstances
> permitted. The Central Gunnery School had its meals at fixed times and
> 'failed to see' why 609 should not do the same. After meal times, the door
> of the dining room was locked. All our efforts to get the Luftwaffe to respect
> the Central Gunnery School meal times having failed, a dead lock occurred.

* Full details of 609 Squadron's kills and losses can be found in Appendices C & D – *Author*

Flight Lieutenant Frank Howell, OC 'A' Flight

In the end, the Mess consented to send our tea and breakfast to the pilot's tent and we cooked our own early breakfast over a primus stove in dispersal. Sergeant Fitzgerald and Corporal Walker did a first class job with the bacon and eggs.

Warmwell's attitude towards 609 Squadron must have improved in the days that followed as over the next five days, 609 was in the forefront of 10 Group's defence in each of the German attacks. The first 'big action of 609's war' occurred on the 11th of August when the Luftwaffe launched a very heavy attack against military targets in the Portland/Weymouth

Lt *Wolf Münchmeyer,*
1/ZG 2

A 'cuppa' after ops – centre and facing camera is David Crook, to his right is Squadron Leader Horace Darley

area.* This time, both 'A' and 'B' Flights managed to intercept the Messerschmitt Bf 110 escort at 23,000 feet over Weymouth Bay. With Squadron Leader Darley at their head, 'B' Flight flew straight across a circle of 110s taking full deflection shots, each section then breaking up and selecting individual targets. This was the sight that met 'A' Flight. Still waiting for their blooding, Flight Lieutenant Frank Howell led his flight into the fray, adding to both the confusion and mêlée. David Crook, having seen his victim's engine catch fire and stall and then having to avoid colliding with the German fighter, found himself below the main action and on looking-up reported seeing 'a terrific fight' and decided that he was a prime candidate for being bounced so headed back to Warmwell to refuel and rearm.

Back at Warmwell, 609s groundcrew waited expectantly in the hope that all of their pilots would return. In one's and two's, their Spitfires were spotted descending over the airfield's perimeter. All returned safely, with only one Spitfire damaged by German gunfire, whilst on the credit side the Squadron claimed five Messerschmitt Bf 110s shot down (although David Crook's kill was later downgraded to a probable). The Squadron's victims all came from *Zerstörergeschwader 2* (ZG 2) who lost six fighters, including that of the *Gruppenkommandeur* of I/ZG 2 *Major* Ernst Ott, with a further five

* This raid was 1/JG 53's first mission against mainland Britain – *Author*

returning to France with various degrees of damage. One of the luckier German pilots was *Leutnant* Wolf Münchmeyer of 1/ZG 2. Even after fifty years, he clearly remembers this day:

> On the 11th of August, we went to Portland and Weymouth escorting Junkers Ju 88s which resulted in the first great air battle with hundreds of aircraft involved. When I was guarded two Messerschmitts in front of me, a Spitfire suddenly attacked from the side, closely followed by a Messerschmitt Bf 109. I tried to avoid a burst of tracer bullets by lifting my port wing but failed. Smoke began pouring from my port engine and I found that I could not keep formation. I suddenly found myself surrounded by Spitfires, left and right. I tried to escape by diving almost vertically at full power knowing that my Messerschmitt was heavier and could dive faster than a Spitfire. I calculated that I reached at least 500 MPH, my air speed indicator going off the clock, but pulled out at sea level without my attackers. I then stopped the port engine and feathered the propeller and headed back for our base at St Aubin. An hour and a half later I landed.

Leutnant Münchmeyer could well have been David Crook's victim as Crook reported hitting the Messerschmitt's port engine, the enemy fighter than rolling over to the starboard. However, in such a confused and massive air battle, this cannot be substantiated.

David Crook later found it amusing to report that Flight Lieutenant 'Butch' McArthur had landed somewhat shaken having shot down one enemy fighter but then spun his Spitfire through 15,000 feet in an attempt to throw off an attacker. Understandably, 'Butch' had felt 'a little unwell' and Crook was pleased to report from then on, he was a much wiser flight commander who never went looking for trouble!

On their return to Middle Wallop, 609's pilots must have retired to the Mess for a few welcome beers or Pimms and all talk must have been about the day's victories. At what time they got to bed is not recorded and if they thought that the following day would be a quiet one, they were wrong.

Just before 1100 hours on Monday the 12th of August, the Squadron was called to readiness. This time, Junkers Ju 88s of KG 51 with another heavy escort of Messerschmitt Bf 109s and 110s had been tasked to attack the radar station at Ventnor on the Isle of Wight and Portsmouth Dockyard. At about 1215 hours, the bombers struck, leaving the escorting fighters circling off the Isle of Wight in the hope of enticing the defending RAF fighters away from the bombers. John Dundas wrote in the Operations Record Book of seeing an enormous circle of Messerschmitt Bf 110s orbiting to the east of the Isle of Wight and that it was left to 'A' Flight to start the fight with a similar combat to the previous day ensuing. Flying straight into the circle of enemy aircraft, 'A' Flight took full beam shots at the German fighters and then broke away downwards. This time it was left to 'B' Flight to pick on individual targets.

Again, the results were good with three Messerschmitt Bf 109s and five Messerschmitt Bf 110s destroyed as well as a mixed bag of fighters and bombers probably destroyed or damaged for three Spitfires with a few bullet holes. An additional non-combat casualty was Pilot Officer David Crook's Spitfire whose wings were damaged during a high speed manoeuvre chasing after one of his victims. The Squadron, which should have been on stand down, flew back to Middle Wallop to make the most of this day of rest.

On their return, the pilots were definitely stood down. Some took advantage of the day's glorious weather and a few beers. In fact, Pilot Officer Neville 'Teeny' Overton and John Dundas had started earlier having landed to refuel and rearm at Tangmere and had a few 'medicinal' Pimms at the Officers' Mess before flying back to base. Three of the pilots, 'Butch' McArthur, Pilot Officer Noel Agazarian and David Crook had been granted a twenty-four hour pass and headed off to London where David Crook was to meet his wife and Michael Appleby who had left earlier that morning before the Squadron had been called to readiness. Despite Crook's car breaking down and being five hours late, all must have laughed and drank away the night 'only a few hours after such a desperate fight' as wrote Crook.

However, after a restful afternoon and night, the following morning's weather was misty and only 'A' Flight managed to fly a few uneventful patrols. Those on twenty-four hour passes were back by mid-morning and at about mid-day the Squadron again flew to Warmwell, refuelled then sat and waited in the gradually improving weather.

Although the RAF was not to know, the 13th of August was designated by the Luftwaffe as *Adlertag* or 'Eagle Day'. Attacks in the morning had been postponed due to the bad weather after the attacking bombers were airborne but the message did not get through to all and the attacks were carried out albeit not as planned. However, these attacks did not affect 609 Squadron and it was not until tea time that their Spitfires were 'scrambled'.

Thirteen Spitfires took off and were ordered to patrol Weymouth at 15,000 feet. Soon, German voices began to be heard over the Spitfires' radio and the tension inside the cramped cockpits began to increase. To the south, a large formation of German aircraft was spotted which turned out to be 'Stukas' escorted by Messerschmitt Bf 110s and Messerschmitt Bf 109s whilst to the east could be seen another formation heading for Southampton.* Briefed to attack Warmwell and Middle Wallop, the Stukas' attack was hampered by bad visibility and more importantly by 609 Squadron. In the space of four minutes, 609 Squadron was to claim ten Stukas from II/StG 2 as destroyed. Even though this unit lost only six Stukas destroyed, the attack was thwarted and as the *Gruppenkommandeur* of II/StG 2, *Major* Walter Ennerccerus, reported, the RAF fighters 'ripped our backs open to the collar'.

Even the escorting fighters came off worse against 609 with 5/JG 53 losing two Messerschmitt Bf 109s to 'B' Flight. One of the victors was 'Novi' Nowierski who by now, together with 'Osti' Ostazewski, was combat ready. As he reported to Flying Officer R J MacKay, the Squadron Intelligence Officer, on his return:

* One of the escorting German fighters operating over Southampton was flown by *Leutnant* Münchmeyer. Shot down by a Hurricane of 601 Squadron, he was destined to spend the remainder of the war as a prisoner – *Author*

I was flying as 'Green Two'. We sighted a large number of enemy aircraft coming from the south. We circled above them and 'Green One' dived to attack. At that moment, I saw an Me 109 above me and ahead. I climbed up behind him and fired three bursts at fairly close range and dead astern. White smoke appeared from his fuselage and he turned over and started to dive. Some large object, probably the cockpit roof or door, flew away and the pilot got out and opened his parachute.

End of the day, Warmwell, 13 August 1940

'Novi' Nowierski with an admirer

A similar report was filed by another member of Green Section, David Crook. He reported that his victim crashed and the pilot was killed. In fact, both German losses survived, *Feldwebel* Hans-Heinz Pfannschmidt was shot down by 'Novi' Nowierski into Weymouth Bay and was captured whilst *Unteroffizier* Willi Hohenfeldt survived being shot down by David Crook when his fighter crashed into the eastern edge of Poole Harbour.

All thirteen RAF pilots returned safely and all but one claimed something. The only pilot not to claim was Squadron Leader Horace Darley but it was his tactical planning and awareness that resulted in such a successful combat with only one Spitfire being lightly damaged. So excited were they and pleased with their success that photographs were taken of all pilots and the score board for the day. Again, as night fell, the 609 pilots retired to the Mess confident that at long last they were a highly effective and cohesive fighting machine. The normal question on the lips of the ground crew seeing their Spitfires return was 'Bags of joy, Sir?' to which the normal answer was 'Yes'. However, August was by no means over as events the following day were to prove.

The following day was an anti-climax for both sides compared to the attacks of *Adlertag*. With the UK covered by cloud, the Luftwaffe did not put in an appearance until later in the afternoon. At about 1600 hours the air raid warning was given in the Southampton area but due to the thick cloud cover the attackers were not identified. Earlier that afternoon about seventeen Junkers Ju 88s of *I/ Lehrgeschwader 1* (I/LG 1) had taken off from their base at Orleans-Bricy with the aim of nuisance attacks against airfields and military targets in the south-west. One of the targets was Middle

Opposite above
Junkers Ju 88s of LG 1 head towards their target, Summer 1940

Opposite below
The damaged hangar with the door that killed

609 poses after the 13 August 1940 combat. Back left to right: Tobin, Ostazewski, Goodwin, Edge, Appleby, Howell, Darley, McArthur, Feary, Nowierski, Overton. Front left to right: Staples, Crook, Miller

Opposite *Retribution –
the remains of the Ju 88
shot down by Sergeant
Feary*

609's groundcrew take shelter

Wallop and at about 1715 hours the first of three Junkers Ju 88s burst out of the cloud, dropped its lethal load and climbed back into the cloud and relative safety.

There was chaos on the ground. Middle Wallop's pitifully inadequate ground defences opened fire on the attacker but to no avail. Bombs exploded around the hangars but one stick of bombs, presumably from the last attacker, did the most damage. A maintenance party made up from 609 Squadron's groundcrew had been trying to close the massive steel doors of Number 5 Hangar to minimise any blast damage. It was as they were doing this that a 250kg bomb entered through the roof and exploded. The blast blew the door off the upper guide rails and it fell on the airmen, killing them instantly.

Unaware of the carnage below, Sergeant Alan Feary, 609's only non-commissioned pilot, who had taken-off earlier together with John Dundas, saw a twin-engined aircraft approaching from the south. As it flew by, he noticed the black crosses on the fuselage and wings. Dundas managed to give it a quick burst before it disappeared into cloud. Alan Feary then dived through the cloud hoping to intercept and at 8,000 feet saw, to his right, a Junkers Ju 88 bombing Middle Wallop. He immediately gave chase and closed to 250 yards behind it and gave a ten second burst. Aboard the German bomber, it must, like Middle Wallop, have been carnage. It began to dive and after a further burst of fire from Feary which finished his ammunition, the German bomber crashed and burst into flames.

One of 609's Spitfires destroyed in the hangar

Debate has arisen whether it was Feary or Sergeant Michael Boddington of 234 Squadron who shot down this aircraft, but according to David Crook, Feary's victim crashed in flames about five miles from the airfield and the Derby-born Alan Feary was given the crew dinghy as a souvenir of his victory.

Back at Middle Wallop, the airfield was trying to recover from the shock. Other Spitfires were scrambled and pilots were put on cockpit readiness but by that time the damage had been done. As well as the maintenance party, three civilian contractors lay dead and about fifteen were wounded. Number 5 Hangar was a wreck and within it, three of 609's Spitfires had been destroyed and another damaged.

However, the air battles in and around Middle Wallop continued. The remainder of 609 Squadron had taken-off without orders and attempted to catch enemy aircraft that were popping in and out of cloud. David Crook succeeded in damaging a Heinkel He 111 which was then finished-off by John Dundas. Briefed to attack the airfields of either Upavon or Netheravon in Wiltshire, the Heinkel shot down by Dundas crashed in the grounds of the Royal Navy Armament Depot at East Dean near Southampton. In the wreckage were the bodies of *Oberst* Alois Stöckl, *Kommodore* of KG 55, *Oberst* Walter Frank, Chief of Staff for *V Fliegerkorps*

One of 604's Blenheims destroyed in the hangar

A near miss

and *Oberleutnant* Bruno Brossler, KG 55's navigation specialist. Surprisingly, two crew survived but the loss of this bomber and crew must have been a serious loss for the Luftwaffe. An amusing, but luckily not serious, combat also took place between one of 609's pilots and a friendly aircraft. Blenheims of 604 Squadron had also taken off after the raid in the hope that they might be lucky in shooting down one of the enemy. However, in the gloom, Flying Officer John Newbery was to mistake the twin-engined Blenheim for a Junkers 88 and a brief exchange of fire took place between the Spitfire and the Blenheim's rear gunner. By luck or bad marksmanship, both missed each other and returned embarrassed to Middle Wallop.

Sadly, one of the Spitfires failed to return. Flying Officer Henry 'Mac' Goodwin had taken-off and nothing more was either heard or seen of him. However, at 1814 hours an RAF fighter was seen to crash in the sea two miles south of Boscombe Pier in Dorset. The pilot baled out and although a lifeboat was sent out, he could not be found. Some ten days later, 'Mac's' body was washed ashore on the Isle of Wight and he was buried in a quiet Worcestershire church yard alongside his brother, Pilot Officer B L Goodwin who had been killed in a flying accident on the 24th of June 1940. 609 had lost not only its first pilot in the hectic month of August 1940 but also three of its devoted ground crew all of which had a sobering effect on the Squadron pilots despite the two successes of that day; any socialising on that night must have been muted.

Opposite above
*View out of the hangar –
the airborne interception
aerials are just about
visible on the wing of the
604 Squadron Blenheim
in the background*

Opposite below
*A brave cameraman
photographs one of the
German bombs exploding*

*Goodwin's Spitfire –
serial N3024 coded PR-
H, shot down 14 August
1940*

*609's groundcrew prepare
to clear up after the attack
on Middle Wallop*

Flying Officer 'Mac' Goodwin

Unexploded bombs are detonated

The following day started quietly at Middle Wallop. The ground crews ensured that their Spitfires were ready for whatever the Luftwaffe was going to throw at them, whilst around the airfield, personnel were clearing up the damage from I/LG 1's attack. However, Thursday the 15th of August 1940 was to be the day the Luftwaffe flew nearly 2,000 sorties against the United Kingdom from as far north as Dundee down to the south-west of England and became known to those Luftwaffe aircrew that took part as *Schwartzdonnerstag* – 'Black Thursday'. Yet again, it was not until later in the afternoon that 609 Squadron came to readiness as radar picked up a massive formation heading for the Southampton area.

Earlier in the morning of the 15th, the Messerschmitt Bf 110s of II/ZG 76 moved from their airfield at Le Mans to the Channel Islands. The weather forecast for the afternoon was good and the task of II/ZG 76 was to escort the Junkers Ju 88s of I/LG 1 in an attack on Middle Wallop. At the same time, II/LG 1 would be attacking the airfield of Worthy Down* whilst the Stukas of I & II/StG 1 and II/StG 2 would be attacking military targets in the Portland area, all designed to stretch Fighter Command's resources to the limit. As normal, there was a massive fighter escort made up of both Messerschmitt Bf 109s and 110s.

The attack on Middle Wallop was scheduled for early in the afternoon but it was not until about 1600 hours that II/ZG 76 took off in Staffel strength from the airfield at Guernsey. Tucked in behind the fighter of the *Staffelkapitän* of 6/ZG 76, *Hauptmann* Heinz Nacke, *Feldwebel* Jakob Birndorfer and his radio operator *Unteroffizier* Max Guschewski commented to each other on how beautiful and sunny the afternoon had become but were concerned that there were no clouds in which to hide if attacked. Reaching their designated altitude, they met up with I/LG 1 and, with the escort taking positions to the left, right and behind the bombers, the whole armada headed for Middle Wallop.

On crossing the coast between Portland and the Isle of Wight, Max Guschewski spotted that they were being stalked by three RAF fighters who were trying to gain altitude. Unmolested so far, the formation reached Middle Wallop from the south, over-flew the target and turned west so as to attack out of the sun. Guschewski saw fighters taking-off from Middle Wallop 'in a most hectic manner' and knew that they were going to have a fight on their hands.

Meanwhile on the ground, most of 609 Squadron had managed to get airborne before the first bombs were dropped and David Crook reported seeing Junkers Ju 88s dive out of the sun, drop their bombs and head for the Coast at full throttle. Flight Lieutenant Frank Howell borrowed one of 'B' Flight's Spitfires and managed to get the undercarriage up and hare away as the first bombs exploded at about 1738 hours. Number 5 Hangar was hit again as well as Number 4 and the motor transport petrol pumps. Other bombs fell near the Sergeants' Mess and 609's accommodation but

---

* Although correctly identified as an airfield, Worthy Down had no involvement in the air defence of the United Kingdom and further illustrates the Luftwaffe's incomplete intelligence of Fighter Command – *Author*

One of 6/ZG 76's shark-
mouthed Messerschmitt Bf
110s

Hptm *Nacke's
Messerschmitt Bf 110C
photographed by his
wingman. Nacke was the
StKap of 6/ZG 76*

the only damage sustained was that all of the windows were blown out in these buildings. The damage, considering the number of bombs, was slight in comparison to the previous day's attack.

Almost immediately after the bombers had released their load, the RAF fighters attacked. To the rear of the formation, 6/ZG 76 turned to fight. Jakob Birndorfer tried to cover his *Staffelkapitän* but as more and more RAF fighters joined in the attack, it became a fight for their lives. Flying Officer 'Osti' Ostazewski had taken off independently of the rest of 609's 'B' Flight and saw the Messerschmitts of 6/ZG 76 in their defensive circle. Flying in the opposite direction to the circle of German fighters, he singled out Jakob Birndorfer's Messerschmitt and gave him a two to three second burst. Jakob Birndorfer dived away, jinking and twisting, whilst Max Guschewski fired drum after drum of ammunition at the attacking fighter. Soon, a second Spitfire joined in. Pilot Officer Jan Zurakowski of 234 Squadron had managed to get airborne the same time as 609's Frank Howell and had also latched on to the unfortunate Messerschmitt. Both Polish pilots now took turns in shooting at the German fighter.

Pilot Officer Piotr Ostazewski

In a vain attempt to throw off their pursers, Birndorfer flew through the Southampton balloon barrage, but to no avail. In the rear of the cockpit, Max Guschewski, now wounded, had run out of ammunition and watched helplessly as the Spitfires came to within five metres of their tail and opened fire. Max Guschewski recalls:

> Bullets were hitting our plane like a hail storm. Even today, after so many years, the terrible noise remains in my ears. It was a sound that can only be described as if somebody was throwing gravel into a tin bowl.

Even Jan Zurakowski can clearly remember the combat after fifty years:

> I attacked many times, firing short bursts. After every attack, I was breaking away and hoped that the Messerschmitt would crash. The fuselage of the German fighter had many holes in it as if someone had sat on it hacking it with an axe.

Getting lower and lower, 'Osti' Ostazewski was still also attacking the German. The port engine caught fire as the Messerschmitt burst out of the balloon barrage and approaching the Isle of Wight, 'Osti' saw the starboard engine smoke and stop and the Messerschmitt began losing height. The last volley had wounded Max Guschewski again and had fatally wounded his pilot; the last thing that Max Guschewski remembers is Jakob Birndorfer throwing off what was left of the cabin roof and giving the order to bale out. Guschewski then passed out and shortly afterwards, the Messerschmitt hit the ground at a shallow angle, bounced back up in the air and, on hitting the ground a second time, skidded to a halt and started to burn. Satisfied and out of ammunition, both Spitfires flew back to Middle Wallop but did not see Max Guschewski manage to stagger out of his broken fighter and collapse a short distance away. In the Messerschmitt, Jakob Birndorfer lay dead.

609 Squadron harried the German force back out across the Channel claiming a total of five aircraft destroyed. For one of the successful pilots, it was a fitting end to his time on 609 Squadron. One of the few remaining pre-war Auxiliaries, it was decided to post Flying Officer 'Grandpa' Edge to 5 Service Flying Training School as an instructor and for a well deserved rest, the combat of the 15th of August being his last both with the Squadron and for the war. His parting shot, so to speak, was to shoot down a Messerschmitt Bf 110 near Romsey, probably the one that crashed into the grounds of Broadlands, the home of Lord Louis Mountbatten.

Again, Blenheims of 604 Squadron had taken to the air during the attack and again, 609 Squadron took an unintentional dislike to that Squadron. David Crook was not aware that Sergeant Cyril Haigh's Blenheim had latched on to the rear of the German formation and as Crook gained on the Germans, he fired at the first twin-engined aircraft he saw. Hitting both engines, the Blenheim broke away and only then did Crook see a turret on the top of the fuselage. However, Crook's aim was good and the Blenheim limped back to crash-land at Middle Wallop, its gunner, Sergeant Walter Fenton, having been wounded in his backside. Considerable embarrassment was experienced by both Squadrons but luckily, the 'combat' had not had fatal consequences.

Flying Officer 'Grandpa' Edge (seen here as a Wing Commander at the end of the war)

The days that followed were quieter for 609 Squadron. During the next eight days the Squadron was scrambled a number of times without any contact. However, the occasional minor accidents occurred, the most amusing and worth mentioning occurring on the 18th of August. As wrote Flight Sergeant Cloves:

> Air Raid warning – again, no raiders or contact with the enemy. Pilot Officer Keough landing off patrol struck a dispersed Blenheim. Flaps and tail unit of the Spitfire damaged but not too seriously. The Blenheim? We did not dare ask, our name was mud on the Blenheim Squadron.

Yet again, 604 Squadron had come off worse!

The Squadron was next in action on the 24th of August but this has been covered in a previous chapter, as has the combats fought on the following day. The only events worth mentioning that occurred in the closing days of the month was that both Air Commodore The Duke of Kent (or as Pilot Officer 'Shorty' Keough called him – 'the Dook') and Marshal of the RAF Lord Trenchard paid a visit to Middle Wallop and the Squadron whilst Pilot Officer Andy Mamedorf tried to make amends for being shot down on the 24th by having a 'squirt' at a Messerschmitt Bf 109 on the 26th of August and failed miserably.

To John Dundas, who wrote the preamble to August's Operations Record Book entries, was left the job of the concluding entry of this month. He wrote:

> It will be seen from the postings to the Squadron during this month that the Squadron was becoming cosmopolitan. One might think that this hetero-geneity would interfere with team work or morale but this was not so. Under Squadron Leader Darley's quietly firm and competent leadership, this Squadron gained steadily in skill and confidence and remained a veritable 'Band of Brothers'. That this sentiment was not confined to the pilots but was reciprocally shared by the ground staff . . .

In response to a letter written by the groundcrew to their Commanding Officer and pilots, Squadron Leader Horace Darley summed up the month of August by writing:

> On behalf of the pilots of this Squadron, I thank you for your words of appreciation of our efforts.
> Our results can only be achieved by confidence in our aircraft and it is due to your hard work and skill that the engines have kept going, the bullets have found their mark and that the air is filled with SORBO* war whoops.
> Keep going hard with all your skill and might for I shall have to ask you to keep up and increase this pace before this show is finally over.

The show was nowhere near over and as August rolled into September, 609 Squadron's work pace, successes and losses were to increase.

---

* SORBO was 609 Squadron's callsign in the air – *Author*

CHAPTER FIVE

Yet Another Big Field Day

September opened quietly as far as we were concerned and though we did
a number of patrols, nothing much happened . . .

So wrote David Crook. Although still carrying out the orders of the
Second Phase attacks attempting to emasculate Fighter Command, the
Luftwaffe began to concentrate its efforts against targets in 11 Group's
area. Pilot Officer John Bisdee recorded in his logbook that flights for the
first six days of September consisted of patrols over Northolt and towns
such as Guildford, Maidenhead and Windsor. As wrote Flight Sergeant
Cloves:

Nothing of account happened; there seemed to be a lull. The Squadron
invariably patrolled Northolt, Brooklands and Windsor daily but didn't see
a sausage.

The only incident of note during this period was that the only American
pilot who had not blotted his copybook by having an accident in his Spitfire
did so when Pilot Officer Andy Mamedorf burst a tyre on landing returning
from a patrol on the 3rd of September. He then hit a ridge and nosed
over. The result? A new airscrew and Mamedorf had completed the 'Hat
Trick of American Prangs'. Even 609's new Canadian pilot, Pilot Officer
Keith Ogilvie, who had been posted in as a replacement following the
death of 'Mac' Goodwin, thought that as he was a Canadian, he
would be neighbourly and follow the lead of the USA. He too burst a
tyre on landing and somehow managed to write off both wings in the
inevitable crash.

In addition to these uneventful patrols, training still continued with a few
hair raising results. Flying Officer John Dundas failed to write in the
Record Book that whilst landing after night flying, he hit an anti-aircraft
gun which, apart from terrifying the gun crew, snapped off one of his
carriage legs which landed on another gun post! In the ensuing crash-
landing, he all but wrote-off his Spitfire.

Nevertheless, on Saturday the 7th of September, things were about to
change for the worse. The Luftwaffe, thinking that their attacks in the 11
Group area had succeeded in reducing the RAF's capability of defending
London, decided to throw its full strength against the United Kingdom's
capital. It was to turn out to be 609's first big action for nearly two weeks.

In the morning the Squadron had carried out its usual patrol in the
Brooklands area. Low on fuel and having seen no enemy, they returned

to Middle Wallop. However, while patrolling Brooklands and Windsor later in the afternoon, the Squadron was amazed to see a formation of more than 200 German fighters and bombers, surrounded by anti-aircraft fire, flying over the city. At full throttle and full boost, Flight Lieutenant 'Butch' McArthur, who was leading the Squadron, climbed away from the patrol line and headed 609 towards the mass of aircraft.

One Canadian (Pilot Officer Ogilvie) and one American (Pilot Officer Tobin)

What followed was a confused air battle. Sergeant Alan Feary reported seeing German aircraft everywhere he looked, not sure which one to attack. However, he probably destroyed a Messerschmitt Bf 109 and damaged a Junkers Ju 88. Flight Lieutenant Frank Howell watched a Messerschmitt Bf 110, its wing ripped away by another RAF fighter, cartwheel away downwards in slow motion whilst another exploded in front of him, bits and pieces of aircraft flying in every direction.

With such a large number of aircraft, casualties were inevitable. However, the now wise and no longer over confident McArthur succeeded in getting 609's Spitfires into the battle and out again claiming six aircraft destroyed and others damaged and probably destroyed without any loss to themselves. Pilot Officer Noel Agazarian did have to land at White Waltham having been hit by return fire from a German bomber while two other Spitfires were found to have a few holes in them on their return to Middle Wallop. The Squadron's Spitfires, low on fuel, landed at the nearest airfield to refuel and rearm and in one's and two's, managed to get back to base before considered being overdue. It was a happy bunch of RAF pilots who turned up at the actor Gordon Harker's cocktail party that evening. Yet again good team work paid off and the Squadron's score of enemy aircraft was rising rapidly.

The days that followed contained the usual patrols in the usual areas but, hampered by bad weather, the Luftwaffe failed to lock horns with 609 Squadron. 'Whatever went on did not seem to concern us,' reported Flight Sergeant Cloves. This situation didn't last and the good weather on Sunday the 15th of September brought the Luftwaffe out in force in what has become regarded as the climax of the Battle of Britain. John Dundas wrote in the Operations Record Book 'Another big field day over London' for indeed it was but for one of 609's pilots who awoke, on that bright Sunday morning, he was destined never to see the sun set again.

The day started quietly and the Squadron was not scrambled until about 1130 hours when they were ordered to patrol to the west of London. At about 1215 hours they were ordered south-east and, over Kenley, waded into a formation of Dornier Do 17s, presumably from KG 76. What happened afterwards is vague but the most spectacular kill was credited to a Canadian Pilot Officer, Keith Ogilvie. Although claimed by a number of other pilots – a fact admitted by the Canadian pilot, the Dornier Do 17 attacked by him (from 1/KG 76) broke up over central London; the main wreckage falling on Victoria Railway Station. One of the Dornier's wings landed outside a public house in Pimlico 'to the great joy and comfort of the patrons' reported the Squadron Operations Record Book. *Oberleutnant* Robert Zehbe, the pilot of the Dornier, and two of his crew were killed but

The Dornier Do 17 at Victoria Station

*One of the RAF pilots
who was responsible for
its demise, Keith Ogilvie
relaxes shortly after the
combat by reading Daphne
Du Maurier's* Jamaica
Inn

two other crew members succeeded in baling out and were captured. Witnessed by Her Majesty Queen Wilhelmina of the Netherlands, the RAF informed her *Aide de Camp*, Major General de Jonge Van Ellemeet, that Pilot Officer Ogilvie of 609 Squadron was the victorious RAF pilot and de Jonge wrote:

> I am commanded by Her Majesty Queen Wilhelmina of the Netherlands to convey to you that Her Majesty was most gratified to see from her London house a German bomber shot down by an eight-gun fighter during the air battle in the morning of 15th of September.
>
> Her Majesty would be very pleased if her congratulations should be conveyed to the Squadron concerned in this battle and to the pilot who shot down the German plane.

Today, Keith Ogilvie is very modest about his part in shooting down this bomber, preferring to remember how he had to take avoiding action to prevent hitting one of the Germans who baled out in front of him.

The Squadron made its way back to Middle Wallop having accounted for itself very well. Unfortunately, one of its Spitfires was missing and, as the afternoon progressed and no news was received, the Squadron began to expect the worse. Pilot Officer Geoffrey Gaunt, a pre-war auxiliary who in September 1939 was a pupil pilot and fought to be posted back to 609 Squadron in July 1940, was last seen following Pilot Officer Michael Appleby against the Dorniers. What happened next is not known but on the ground near to the village of Addington in Kent, horrified spectators saw a Spitfire fluttering down and hit the ground. The pilot was not seen to bale out. Pilot Officer 'Red' Tobin had seen a Spitfire spin away in an uncontrollable dive and suspected that the pilot was Geoffrey Gaunt but no one knew for sure what had happened to him.

On leave at the time David Crook heard the following day that his friend Geoffrey was missing. He contacted the Squadron but neither he or the Gaunt family could be put out of their misery. It was not until some days later, on the 19th of September, that Squadron Leader Darley was handed a telegram which had arrived from the airfield at Kenley over which the combat on the 15th of September had taken place. It stated that they had found the wreckage of a Spitfire in which they had discovered the remains of its pilot. It was virtually impossible to identify the dead airman but they had found a name sewn on the collar band of his uniform. The name was that of 'Gaunt'.

David Crook was deeply moved by the loss of his friend whom he had known all of his life. In his book, he devotes a number of pages to his late friend ending by saying:

> For me it was the biggest loss that I have ever experienced. I could not believe that such a vital spark was now extinguished for ever and that I would not see him again.

A Dornier Do 17Z of KG 76 takes off on another mission

How the rest of the Squadron felt about the loss of such a popular officer

Pilot Officer Geoffrey Gaunt (Dilip Sarkar Collection)

is not known. The Operations Record Book probably sums up their feelings by saying:

> Gaunt was a good pilot and competent operations officer but even more as a man is his loss deeply regretted.

The Squadron, still hoping that Geoffrey Gaunt would turn up later, was to fly one more sortie on the 15th of September. Again, their quarry were Dornier Do 17s but this time from KG 2 engaging them near Rye as the Germans were returning from their attack on London. Claims are confusing but with no escort, the pilots of 609 squadron picked on two of the stragglers and took great delight in sending one bomber into the sea and the other to crash-land north of Hastings. David Crook was told afterwards that the twelve 609 Squadron Spitfires totally overwhelmed the unfortunate German bombers which were shot to pieces.

609 Squadron must have been exhausted as the sun set on this vital day. Their successes had been marred by the loss of one pilot and only three other casualties had occurred. The less serious were the two Spitfires damaged by enemy gun fire. However, the third aircraft casualty was more serious; again, it was one of the American pilots who was dogged by bad luck. Returning from helping to shoot down one of the Dorniers in the first engagement, Pilot Officer 'Red' Robin was unable to avoid hitting the crash truck that shot out in front of him as he was landing at Middle Wallop. With only one wheel, he managed to land the Spitfire and thankfully walk away without injury to himself. Annoyed and without a Spitfire, he was unable to take part in the later combat of the day.

A casualty that almost happened but thankfully did not involved Flight Lieutenant 'Butch' McArthur. During the afternoon's combat, his oxygen failed while flying at about 25,000 feet. After handing over command of the Flight to Michael Appleby, he had blacked out when trying to avoid a passing Messerschmitt Bf 109 that was taking an interest in him. He fortunately recovered at 2,000 feet unaware that he had badly damaged his ears in the process.

The Squadron, by now, had settled into a familiar routine of fighting for their lives one day and having nothing to do in the days that followed and this was true after the 15th of September. On the 16th 'Butch' McArthur flew one of the Spitfires, damaged the day before, to Hamble and yet again, the Hamble jinx struck although this time its victim was not American. On arriving in the circuit, the Spitfire's air speed indication 'went goofy' and on seeing another aircraft approaching to land, 'Butch' decided to follow him in. The pilot of this aircraft did not like the idea of being followed so went around for another circuit. 'Butch' followed him and this went on for a few more circuits before the pilot of the other aircraft decided he had had enough and landed. Following him in, 'Butch' forgot to lower his undercarriage and with a shower of earth, grass and stones, the Spitfire slithered to a stop on its belly. Later, when told that the Spitfire was a write off, 'Butch' was heard to say 'I did not like the thing any way'.

On the 21st, I/LG 1 paid another visit to Middle Wallop with little involvement for 609 Squadron except a lot of shouting. Chased by Hurricanes of 238 Squadron, *Oberleutnant* Kurt Sodemann dropped his bombs at the back of the barrack blocks, watched by some of 609's pilots. Shouting their encouragement and egging on the Hurricanes, they saw the German bomber head off south-east to be eventually shot down near Chichester. Three days later, the Squadron was back in action again.

In the afternoon of the 24th of September, the Luftwaffe began a series of attacks against aircraft factories in the south-west of England. The specialist bombing unit *Erprobungsgruppe 210* flying Messerschmitt Bf 110s modified to carry bombs, carried out a lightning attack on the Supermarine Works at Woolston near Southampton which resulted in the deaths of forty-two workers. No RAF fighter was able to intercept the German Unit. Three hours later, they were back again but this time, there was opposition for them to contend with. 609 had been scrambled and intercepted what they identified as a very mixed formation. Pilots reported combats with Messerschmitt Bf 109s and 110s, Dornier Do 17s and even French Morane fighters. What they did meet was purely Messerschmitt Bf 109s and 110s, the German formation losing three Messerschmitt Bf 110s, while the Squadron claimed four destroyed and three others either damaged or probably destroyed.

A similar attack occurred the following day but now the formation was larger and their target the Bristol Aeroplane Company Works at Filton on the outskirts of Bristol. This time 609 Squadron's score was higher and could have been increased had 10 Group Headquarters got 609 and the

A Messerschmitt Bf 110 Jabo – note the bomb racks beneath the fuselage

other Squadrons into the air quicker. The only 10 Group Squadron on readiness was 609 and at 1120 hours, when the German formation was a mere five miles off Portland, they took to the air. Frustratingly, they were first sent to Portland, then Swanage and then Yeovil, catching up with the German bombers on the outskirts of Bristol thirty-five minutes after getting airborne.

By all accounts, the German formation was impressive. The Heinkel He 111s of KG 55 were so tightly packed that it was impossible to aim at specific aircraft and the concentrated return fire from the German gunners was daunting. However, Squadron Leader Darley again judged the situation correctly and quickly attacked out of the sun in a vain attempt to thwart the German bombers. Sadly, 609 Squadron were unable to prevent the German bombers from releasing their loads and carpet bombing Filton. Within the factory, over ninety people were killed or fatally wounded and over 150 injured. Casualties occurred in Bristol as well with nearly sixty killed and nearly 200 injured. Surprisingly, the factory was not completely destroyed and normal production was resumed a few months later.

It was now 609's job to harry the attacking force all the way back to the coast. Many combats were shared between 609 and other Squadrons such as the kill shared between Pilot Officers Roger Miller and Noel Agazarian and Pilot Officer John Urwin-Mann of 238 Squadron. They all latched onto the Heinkel flown by the *Staffelkapitän* of 7/KG 55, *Oberleutnant* Hans Bröckers. Nearing Poole and mortally damaged, the Heinkel's crew began

A Heinkel He 111 of 3/KG 55

baling out. With its pilot still at the controls, the Heinkel crashed into housing at Branksome Park, Poole. In the wreckage was the body of the German pilot and although the four other crew members baled out, only one survived.

Low on fuel and not wanting to get involved with the Messerschmitt Bf 109s waiting off the coast to escort the Heinkels and Messerschmitt Bf 110s home, 609 headed back for Middle Wallop. Only one of their number failed to return, Sergeant David Hughes Rees' Spitfire had developed engine trouble and force-landed near Glastonbury with little damage to the aircraft and no damage to its pilot. Hughes Rees was a welcome companion for Sergeant Alan Feary, who until his arrival was the only non-commissioned pilot on the Squadron, and he had settled in well. He had arrived a mere week earlier, probably as a replacement for Geoffrey Gaunt, and on the 25th of September had claimed a Dornier Do 215 prior to his Spitfire's engine failing. The ferocity of the air battle can further be illustrated by the fact that two of 609's Spitfires had returned to Middle Wallop with distorted wings and shattered canopies from pulling out of power dives in their keenness to either get at the bombers or get away from the escorting German fighters. One of the pilots, Flying Officer John Newbery, also suffered severe internal injuries through pulling out of the dive which had also resulted in his Spitfire's seat collapsing. He was admitted to hospital and never again flew with the Squadron.

The following day saw yet another attack by KG 55 against Woolston which caused serious disruption to Spitfire production and resulted in their construction being dispersed away from Woolston. Again, 609 Squadron accounted for a number of the enemy despite intercepting after the bombers had attacked their intended target. Sadly, this day saw the departure of Flight Lieutenant 'Butch' McArthur. Suffering from continual problems with his ears when flying at altitude, he had to see a specialist to find out exactly what was wrong. While his Squadron was fighting, he was returning from a medical appointment knowing that he could only remain on operational flying as long as he never flew above 5,000 feet. With most combats well in excess of 5,000 feet, he knew that he could not remain in 609 Squadron and was soon posted to Headquarters 10 Group for a rest tour. Promotion and the award of the DFC soon followed for this popular Flight Commander and his place as 'B' Flight Commander was taken by John Dundas, a very well received choice. Also on the move were the three Americans Tobin, Keough and Mamedorf. They were posted to help form the first 'Eagle' Squadron. The Operations Record Book reported:

> The three American pilots . . . left us with evident reluctance and to our great regret . . . Both in the air and on the ground they had contributed colour, variety and vocabulary to the Squadron and their 'wise cracking' will be missed.

So far, the Luftwaffe attacks had resulted in 609's score nearing the hundred 'kills' mark with, fortunately, few serious casualties. But by now fatigue had started to set in amongst the pilots – they had been on continuous operational and front line tasks since the end of May and despite the initial casualties over Dunkirk and those suffered during the early weeks of the Battle of Britain, losses were mercifully light even if sad to those who remained. From now on, even though the scoring continued, losses would slowly start to mount.

On the morning of the 27th of September, *Luftflotte 3* tasked *Erprobungsgruppe 210* with attacking the Parnall Aircraft Factory at Yate, nine miles north-east of Bristol. Yet again, 10 Group failed to position 609 Squadron correctly and when their aircraft got to altitude and sighted the German fighter bombers they were too far behind them to be able to intercept. The Squadron were obviously annoyed as the diarist, still presumably John Dundas, wrote:

> For the second time in three days, Number 10 Group Control positioned the Squadron so badly that they had little or no chance of catching any of the bombers over the Coast.

To make matters worse, Squadron Leader Darley began to suffer extreme pain in his ears as he was flying with a cold. Additionally the radio in Flight Lieutenant Frank Howell's Spitfire stopped working. Both of these pilots returned to Middle Wallop and command of 'B' Flight was handed to Pilot Officer Roger 'Mick' Miller while John Dundas took command of 'A' Flight. Spotting about fifteen Messerschmitt Bf 110s circling in the area between Warmwell and Blandford Forum, Mick Miller led the Squadron in to attack. What happened next is best described by three eye witnesses:

> We climbed around them, then dived into the middle of the circle. I saw Yellow One collide with a Messerschmitt Bf 110 while executing a beam attack – John Dundas.
>
> The Messerschmitt turned out to get his cannon working on Mick and they hit head on. There was a terrific explosion, a sheet of flame and a column of black smoke. I glimpsed a Spitfire's wing fluttering out and the white of a parachute with something on the end. It was ghastly – Keith Ogilvie.
>
> I was flying just behind Mick and he turned slightly left to attack a 110 which was coming towards him. But the German was as determined as Mick and refused to give way or alter course to avoid this head on attack. Their aggregate speed of closing was at least 600 mph and an instant later they collided. There was a terrific explosion and a sheet of flame and black smoke seemed to hang in the air like a great ball of fire. Many little shattered fragments fluttered down and that was all – David Crook.

Mick Miller had collided with the Messerschmitt Bf 110 flown by *Gefreiter* Georg Jackstedt of 9/ZG 26. Amazingly, Jackstedt managed to extract himself from his rapidly disintegrating fighter and although wounded, managed to open his parachute; this was the parachute with 'something on the end of it' witnessed by Keith Ogilvie. His radio operator was still in the remains of the German fighter when it hit the ground at Piddletrenthide. Mick Miller's broken body was found in whatever was left of his Spitfire which landed in farmland near Chesilbourne.

Stunned by what had just occurred, the rest of the Squadron had little time to reflect on the death of their friend as they tore into the German fighters, breaking up the formation which then headed out to sea hotly pursued by 609's Spitfires. Who shot down whom is as usual confused but the Squadron claimed five destroyed and three probably destroyed or damaged. One of the more spectacular combats was that between a Messerschmitt Bf 110 and David Crook. Crook chased the German fighter out to sea and caught up with it about twenty miles off the coast. A running battle ensued but although damaging it, Crook ran out of ammunition and could only claim the Messerschmitt as damaged. Disgusted, he was about to return to base when he heard Pilot Officer John Bisdee shout: 'OK, OK – help coming!' Bisdee eventually shot the Messerschmitt into the Channel sixty miles off the Dorsetshire Coast. Recent research would indicate that the pilot of this Messerschmitt was possibly *Oberleutnant* Wilhelm-Richard Rössiger, *Staffelkapitän* of *2/Erprobungsgruppe 210* but as a number of RAF pilots claimed shooting down Messerschmitt Bf 110s over the Channel, this can never be confirmed. Rössiger was a great loss to both the Luftwaffe and his Unit which also lost its *Kommandeur, Hauptmann* Martin Lutz in the same attack. So great was this loss that both Rössiger and Lutz were posthumously awarded the Knight's Cross four days later.

Again, on their return, 609 Squadron were able to ponder over the loss of yet another one of their 'associates'. Crook recalls walking to a late lunch that Friday afternoon and that a few hours before, he had sat next to Mick Miller for breakfast and here was he, Crook, sitting at the same

Messerschmitt Bf 110s of ZG 26

table and same chair only this time Mick was lying dead in a Dorsetshire field.

As before, the Squadron then experienced two days of inactivity, sitting and waiting for the Luftwaffe to show which it did on Monday the 30th of September. A bright, gloriously sunny day, the Squadron was scrambled at about 1030 hours to patrol London but half an hour later, they were recalled and landed without firing a shot or even seeing the enemy. Unfortunately, one casualty occurred when Pilot Officer Johnny Curchin taxied into another aircraft at dispersal (incidentally the only aircraft at that time standing on the airfield!) writing-off the airscrew of his Spitfire and the starboard wing of the other. However, as the refuelling bowsers drove up to the aircraft to top up their tanks, they were scrambled again. At about 1130 hours, several enemy formations made up of Messerschmitt Bf 109s of JG 2, 5/JG 53 and ZG 26 flew over the Coast near Weymouth headed north. Some then flew over Bristol and west over Exeter before heading home while some flew back over Bournemouth and Swanage. The purpose of these flights is not clear but was presumably a 'free chase' with the additional intention of reconnoitring the damage to the aircraft factories in the Bristol area and the Westland Aircraft factory near Yeovil, the latter being the next target on the Luftwaffe's list. *Oberleutnant* Franz Fiby, *Gruppenadjutant* of I/JG 2 remembers that he took off from Cherbourg at 1025 hours for an hour long free chase north of Portland with five Messerschmitt Bf 109's but as the route was well outside the range of the 109s, they had to be content with circling off the Needles. It was these German fighters that became 609s intended prey.

Pilot Officer John Bisdee

Led by Flight Lieutenant Frank Howell, as Squadron Leader Darley was
still unfit to fly, twelve Spitfires climbed towards the circling enemy fighters
and, with the sun behind them, bounced an enemy Staffel; the Germans
did not know the Spitfires were there until too late. Michael Appleby drew
first blood:

> I fired on one, saw my ammunition hitting around the pilot's cockpit and
> David Crook was able to say he saw the aircraft blow up.

Seeing Appleby's victim fall to pieces, Crook chased a diving Messerschmitt
Bf 109 and after a withering burst of fire saw it plunge into the sea in flames
off Swanage, its pilot still strapped inside the cockpit. With the sky full of
wheeling fighters, Crook soon latched onto another which was flying full
throttle for France. After a long chase and with Cherbourg clearly visible,
he managed to shoot it down, only later to express regret for his actions
against what he regarded as a sitting duck.

Crook and Appleby were the only pilots on the Squadron to destroy any
enemy aircraft, three other pilots claiming a mix of three Messerschmitts
probably destroyed or damaged. German records only acknowledge two
losses – *Gefreiter* Fritz Schuhmacher of 5/JG 2 being shot down south of
the Isle of Wight and *Feldwebel* Wilhelm Hermes of 2/JG 2 who was last
seen in the Dorchester area. However, it is also possible that 5/JG 53 lost
one aircraft, its pilot being rescued by German air sea rescue and it is
this aircraft that could have been Crook's second victim. *Oberleutnant*   Oblt *Franz Fiby of*
Fiby remembers that they were involved in combat with Spitfires and   *JG 2*

Hurricanes and he claimed one, his *Gruppenkommandeur*, *Hauptmann* Helmut Wick, another two, but these were not from 609 Squadron and were probably the Hurricanes of Sergeant Ronald Way and Pilot Officer Kenneth Marston of 56 Squadron, both of whom survived.*

Overjoyed with their success, the exhilarated pilots must have expected a quieter afternoon but as usual, the Squadron had its customary tea time scramble. A heavily escorted forty-three Heinkel He 111's of KG 55 were again after another aircraft factory – Westlands at Yeovil. 609 Squadron were given the task of tackling the fighters but outmanoeuvred and outnumbered, only three pilots made contact and of those, only one, Flying Officer 'Novi' Nowierski, got a confirmed kill:

> I was on orders from 'Green Leader', Pilot Officer Crook, to investigate six bogies. They were Messerschmitt 109s. I attacked one from astern and gave him a short burst. I gave him another at the same range. White smoke came from the enemy aircraft and then very thick black smoke and he began to dive steeply. I noticed another in my sights and attacked from astern. I gave him one burst. White and black smoke came from the enemy aircraft. I broke away and after a few seconds, saw a man come down on a parachute which did not open. The parachute seemed to be fouled by a cord half way up.

609's only kill of the afternoon crashed near the village of Sydling St Nicholas in Dorset, the body of the pilot, *Gefreiter* Alois Dollinger of 5/JG 2, falling alongside the wreckage.

The accolades for the day went entirely to 'B' Flight with four of their number having a semi-celebratory dinner in Winchester that night. For Crook, it had been one of the best days he had ever had on the Squadron and this is reflected in the detailed way he wrote about the day in his diary. September had been an eventful month with the Luftwaffe failing to achieve much from their attack on Great Britain. The month that followed heralded yet another Phase and another change in tactics. For the RAF, October and the months leading up to 1941 were an anti-climax. 609 Squadron was to share in this anti-climax but also experienced a number of changes, continued successes and a number of very tragic losses.

* Both *Hauptmann* Helmut Wick and *Oberleutnant* Fiby were to meet 609 Squadron again nearly two months later. On this occasion, the results on both sides were to be totally different – *Author*

CHAPTER SIX

I've Finished a 109, Whooppee!

The final Phase of the Battle of Britain saw the Luftwaffe arming its fighter aircraft with a single 250kg bomb and operating at altitudes in excess of 25,000 feet. With its two stage supercharger, these fighter bombers or *Jabos* had a markedly better performance than the defending RAF fighters. Furthermore, at heights in excess of 20,000 feet, radar and Observer Corps plotting was difficult. Finally, with these fighters not flying at the speeds dictated by the bombers they had been escorting in the previous month, this gave Fighter Command even less time to get its fighters to altitude to intercept. However, 10 Group was outside the range of such *Jabos* and 609 Squadron had to be content with the occasional bomber raids and aggressive Luftwaffe fighter sweeps.

Sadly, on the 4th of October, 609 Squadron had to say goodbye to the architect of their Battle of Britain successes to date. Squadron Leader Horace 'George' Darley was posted on promotion to Wing Commander to command the fighter station at Exeter. He had commanded the Squadron for just over three months and had changed them from a 'miserable and ignorant lot' to what Frank Ziegler, later 609s Intelligence Officer and author of the book chronicling the Squadron's history, described as 'a Squadron second to none'. Darley had been detested by many after his arrival but on his departure, and on realising what he had done for them, many were in tears to see him go. 609 Squadron's fourth Commanding Officer was awarded the Distinguished Service Order (DSO) on the 22nd of October and in response to a letter of congratulation sent by the Squadron said, modestly:

> I thank you all for your extremely kind letter but hasten to assure you that your congratulations are entirely misdirected. The award is due to the whole Squadron, pilots, NCOs and airmen who all backed me up whatever I asked them to do. Please convey my gratitude to them all.

The final accolade for Darley is best summed up by what was written in the Operations Record Book and must have said what the whole Squadron thought of him:

> Darley's honour was nevertheless well earned as an individual award: if the Squadron had indeed played up to him . . . , this was a natural response to first class leadership and personal example. Darley assumed command of the Squadron just after it had gained only moderate success at rather heavy cost in the Dunkirk Evacuation period and morale was none too good. As was

natural for an Auxiliary squadron with a tradition of promotion within the unit, the incursion of a regular Commanding Officer was not hailed with immediate enthusiasm but any disappointments were short lived. Darley had none of the physical attributes of the natural leader of imaginative fiction. At first glance, he could pass for a wizened schoolboy; he said very little as often not in abrupt and half-articulated mumblings. But he demonstrated from the very first that he was a master of his calling, that he expected and required high standards of professional conscience from all ranks and that he asked for no severities of discipline which he was not prepared himself to submit. He was not slow to recognise that he had first class human material on and with which to work. During his command, if the morale of a Squadron could be plotted on a graph, it would describe a rising parabola. Darley left the Squadron with a rare spirit of 'Tails Up'.

Many expected command of the Squadron to pass to Flight Lieutenant Frank Howell but it was in fact given to Squadron Leader Michael Robinson who came across from 238 Squadron, based at the nearby airfield of Chilbolton. Some were disappointed in this choice others were to view their new and somewhat flamboyant Commanding Officer with suspicion and dislike. However, Frank Howell was destined to command a squadron (118 Squadron) some four months later and the attitudes of the majority soon changed for the better towards Squadron Leader Robinson.

October 1940 had started quietly for the Squadron which was fortunate especially with the series of farewell parties and drinks for their old Commanding Officer. On the morning of the 5th of October, Wing Commander Darley bade a fond farewell and the Squadron both settled down and re-adjusted to their new 'Boss'. The following day, the 6th of October, two new, yet familiar, faces arrived on the Squadron from 234 Squadron which although with 609 at Middle Wallop in August was now based at St Eval in Cornwall. The ranks of Polish airmen were swelled with Pilot Officers Jan Zurakowski (the same pilot that shared the destruction of a Messerschmitt Bf 110 with Flying Officer 'Osti' Ostazewski on the 15th of August) and Pilot Officer Zbigniev Olenski (nicknamed by Keith Ogilvie 'Big Enough').

The first 'action' of the month, excluding Flying Officer 'Novi' Nowierski baling out of his Spitfire on a practice flight on the 5th and the Luftwaffe ruining 609's day of rest on the 6th when it bombed the airfield at lunchtime and caused a number of pilots to spill their beer, occurred on Monday the 7th of October. It was to be, as the Operations Record Book recorded:

> . . . a partly successful day but rather expensive . . .

The morning was quiet and compared to the very poor weather of the previous day, the 7th was much better and many on the Squadron suspected that it might entice the Luftwaffe their way. Scrambled at 1530 hours, again just before tea time, 609 Squadron found the visibility to be near perfect with Cornwall just about visible to the west and the Channel Islands visible to the south. Fast approaching and currently unseen in the glare of the sun were twenty Junkers Ju 88s of II/KG 51, escorted by thirty-

Squadron Leader Michael Robinson

Another new pilot − Pilot Officer Olenski

nine Messerschmitt Bf 110s of ZG 26 and fifty-nine Messerschmitt Bf 110s of JG 2 and II/JG 53. Their target was yet another aircraft factory but one that had been visited before − Westlands at Yeovil in Somerset. Over Weymouth at about 1545 hours, 609 spotted the formation and prepared to attack but a warning shout of enemy fighters above resulted in Spitfires and Hurricanes breaking in all directions. What followed was the usual confused combat.

Squadron Leader Robinson on his first sortie with his new Squadron fared well against the defending German fighters, claiming two destroyed. Interestingly, one of his victims crashed on farmland near Long Bredy in Dorset taking with it both of its crew. In 1976, aviation archaeologists recovered the remains of this German fighter and with it the bodies of the German crew who were subsequently reburied with full military honours at the German Military Cemetery at Cannock Chase in Staffordshire.

In total, the Squadron claimed five fighters destroyed and a further two probably destroyed or damaged. However, as intimated in the Operations Record Book entry, the cost to the Squadron was to be their heaviest to date. Sergeant Alan Feary was probably bounced by one of JG 2's fighters and his Spitfire was seen to break downwards, out of control. Struggling hard to regain control and with the probable intention of landing at Warmwell, he succeeded in righting the Spitfire only to have his fighter go into a spin. By the time he recovered from this, his Spitfire was dangerously low and sensing the futility of saving his crippled fighter, he baled out. Sadly, he had left it too late and his parachute failed to deploy fully. His body, shrouded by his parachute, was discovered close to the remains of his Spitfire less than a mile from the airfield at Warmwell. Later that evening, his Squadron was informed that his body had been found and taken to Warmwell. As a tribute, the Operations Record Book said:

> Sergeant A N Feary was a steady painstaking pilot . . . He seemed to regard his Spitfire with the kind of jealous care and affection that some bestow upon animals and the notion has been advanced by those who knew him that this trait in his character may have contributed to the loss of his life, causing reluctance to bale out from a spin which he was unable to control.

He was by no means the only 609 Squadron casualty but thankfully the remainder were not fatal. Pilot Officer Michael Staples was bounced by a Messerschmitt Bf 109 and wounded in his knee, with his Spitfire on fire, he baled out successfully from 21,000 feet. Admitted to hospital, he never flew again with the Squadron. Flight Lieutenant Frank Howell's victim managed to hit his Spitfire's engine with a particularly accurate burst of fire and when the engine seized, he was forced to crash-land near

The Intelligence Officer, Pilot Officer Mackay debriefs Sergeant Alan Feary after a mission

Shaftesbury. Following his 'capture' by both the local police and inhabitants who poured beer down his throat for the next four hours, he was returned to Middle Wallop later that evening the worse for wear. John Dundas was, however, acknowledged as the 'coolest' casualty. Following a wound received when a 20mm shell exploded in his Spitfire's wing, he landed at Warmwell and walked unaided to the Sick Quarters to have his wounds dressed. Typically, his wound did not prevent him from declaring himself fit to fly and fight the following day.

The days that followed were much quieter apart from the announcement on the 9th of October that Flight Lieutenants 'Butch' McArthur and Frank Howell and Flying Officer John Dundas had each been awarded the DFC. Surprisingly, little mention is made of these awards in the Operations Record Book or in the diaries of David Crook and Flight Sergeant Cloves. Being the first such awards of the Battle of Britain (Squadron Leader Darley's being the DSO) and the first since the posthumous award of 609 Squadron's first DFC to Flying Officer Russell back in June 1940, the celebrations should have been worth a mention.

Six days later found the Squadron in a mid-day scramble against a formation of Messerschmitt Bf 109s and Bf 110s and in a similar position to that which they experienced back on the 24th of August – way below the German fighters and, outlined against the cloud – a perfect target. When the inevitable bounce came, it was David Crook who screamed the warning. The Squadron broke in all directions but three pilots struck back, claiming three destroyed. The only one that can be positively confirmed was the victim of Flying Officer 'Novi' Nowierski. Losing the Messerschmitt Bf 109 he had attacked in cloud, it was Pilot Officer Zbigniev Olenski that saw it crash. The pilot, *Gefreiter* Alois Pollach of 4/JG 2, managed to bale out at a very low altitude near Lymington and was spotted, much to the annoyance of the Poles, as having survived and was last seen lying next to his crashed fighter.

The 'kills' on the 15th of October were very important to the Squadron. In the dispersal hut was a pad of numbers from which, on this day, three were torn off. The one that now remained was number '100' indicating that 609 Squadron's next 'kill' would be its hundredth. Tension was mounting, not helped by the lack of Germans in the days that followed. Not even the well deserved awards of the DFC to Pilot Officers David Crook and Johnny Curchin on the 18th of October and the riotous party that followed could break the tension.

However, the 'kill' was inevitable and was to come three days later. In poor weather, Flight Lieutenant Frank Howell and Pilot Officer Sydney Hill were scrambled to intercept a lone enemy bomber which had been plotted over the Midlands and was now headed south. Allegedly posing as a Blenheim, *Oberleutnant* Max Fabian and his three man crew in a Junkers Ju 88 of 1/KG 51 had been machine-gunning Old Sarum airfield near Salisbury when the two Spitfires were skilfully vectored onto it. Still not sure and confused by one of the gunners setting off signal flares in their direction, Frank Howell got closer and on seeing German markings, commenced the attack. At tree-top level, the Spitfires chased the German bomber in a

The CO finds out what happened immediately after the 100th kill – left to right: Sidney Hill, John Dundas, Piotr Ostazewski, Keith Ogilvie, Frank Howell and Michael Robinson

Groundcrew return with bits of the 100th kill

John Curchin and Keith Ogilvie with the most impressive trophy from the 100th kill

thrilling combat. Inevitably, with one engine damaged by Howell, the chances of escape for *Oberleutnant* Fabian were slim and the *coup de grace* was finally given by Sydney Hill who had only been on the Squadron for about three weeks. The Junkers Ju 88 dived into the ground not too far from 609's ninety-ninth kill near Lymington and exploded, killing the crew instantly.

The pilots, on landing back at Middle Wallop, found the preparations for the hundredth 'kill' party to be in full swing. As the two Spitfires landed and taxied in, excited pilots waited for the two victors while a party of ground crew were off to plunder the wreckage of the German bomber for souvenirs, returning with the tail swastika, oxygen bottles and a dive brake. Presumably released for the rest of the day, the first party was for all ranks and held at dispersal whilst a second part was held in the Officers' Mess later that evening. All that David Crook said of the party was that 'it was very good'. No doubt there were many who would have disagreed with that sentiment the following morning!

The month was coming to a close and the tempo of operational flying began to slow down. On the 27th of October, two days before the 'Century Celebration Dinner', the third and final hundredth kill celebration, Green Section fought the last combat of the month with almost fatal consequences. Again vectored skilfully onto a Junkers Ju 88 making use of the bad weather, the German gunners managed to damage the Spitfire of Pilot Officer Paul Baillon, another new pilot posted on the same day as Sydney Hill, causing him to bale out, his Spitfire crashing and bursting into flames

SALVED FROM
JU. 88.
THE 100TH ENEMY AIRCRAFT
SHOT DOWN BY 609 (F) SQUADRON
21ST OCT., 1940
F/LT. HOWELL. D.F.C.
AND
P/O. S. J. HILL.

on the edge of the airfield at Upavon in Wiltshire. Luckily, Paul Baillon landed safely and was able to make the Celebration Dinner two nights later.

The Battle of Britain was finished and 609 Squadron had acquitted itself very well as they now had a total of one hundred kills to their name and had lost remarkably few pilots in comparison to other fighter Squadrons. With the onset of winter the Luftwaffe began to slow down its aerial assault but for the Squadron, the year was by no means over. It was to fly very few combat sorties compared to previous months and its kill tally would increase slightly. Sadly, so would its losses.

After the relatively quiet but alcoholic days at the end of October, the whole Squadron, whose callsign had now changed from SORBO to PERKY took off on the first day of November 1940 in the hope of adding to their score of one hundred kills. But, apart from seeing the Messerschmitt Bf 109s of JG 2 bouncing 213 Squadron, their luck was out. This run of bad luck was to continue until the month was nearly over.

With the pace now slowing, personnel began to be posted out and new, inexperienced pilots began to arrive. The first to go were David Crook and Michael Appleby, posted to the Central Flying School at Upavon on the 9th of November and 24th of November respectively. Both were pre-war auxiliaries and would be sadly missed. Compared to those who were posted before them, very little was written about these stalwarts probably due to John Dundas no longer being the pilot tasked to write the Operations Record Book entries. The only auxiliary now left was in fact John Dundas who was promoted to Fight Lieutenant on the 6th of November (backdated to the 6th of October when he had taken command of 'B' Flight). He must have wondered, seeing the departures of his friends, where he would end up.

With the departures of these pilots, new pilots soon arrived. Many, such as Pilot Officer 'Joe' Atkinson and Sergeant 'Goldy' Palmer were to play an active part in the Squadron history in the months and in some case years to follow. However, for the moment, they were happy to learn from the older hands how to survive in combat and with the reluctance of the Luftwaffe to fight, and bad weather, training became of paramount importance.

Those who had been in the thick of the fighting used this lack of activity to get a leave pass and a well deserved rest. Transport to and from their leave destinations was assisted by the arrival, courtesy of their Commanding Officer, of two 'things'. These 'things' were drones, basically a glider with an engine which would fly at speeds of forty-five to fifty-five mph making more noise than a North American Harvard trainer. Camouflaged and coded PR-? and PR-!, they were a welcome if not official addition to the Squadron establishment.

A stream of visitors now came and paid homage to the Squadron. Marshal of the Air Force Lord Trenchard visited and gave an amazing pep talk which included a warning about winter flying, quite apt considering that the Squadron was due to move to Warmwell towards the end of the month and this airfield held no fond memories for the Squadron. Another

Two of the new pilots –
Sergeant Boyd

and Sergeant Mercer

visitor was war artist Captain Cuthbert Orde. Captain Orde became famous for his sketches of Battle of Britain fighter pilots and copies of the sketches featuring Squadron members now hang in the Air Terminal at the present RAF base at Northolt, at Leeds Bradford Airport (formerly Yeadon, 609's first home) and in the 609 (West Riding) Squadron Museum at the Yorkshire Air Museum near York.

It was not until exactly a month after the last combat that 609 Squadron was to fire its guns in anger again. In poor weather, operations reported that a Junkers Ju 88 was headed home along the Coast. Flight Sergeant Cloves takes up the account:

> Flight Lieutenant Dundas asked if he could take a section and chase it. He was told 'No, it's too far away' or some such reply. He then asked if he could have permission for a section to do practice flying which was granted. On becoming airborne, he broke away from his section and began to stalk the Junkers Ju 88. He chased it over to Cherbourg and gave it the works. The Junkers disappeared in smoke but he (Dundas) could not stop to confirm it being very close to an aerodrome loaded with Me 109s.

Though he had only damaged his opponent, John Dundas had proved a point and as he went to bed that night must have been quite satisfied with himself. He was to have no idea what the following day would bring.

On the other side of the Channel early in the afternoon of Thursday the 28th of November 1940, *Oberleutnant* Franz Fiby, the *Gruppenadjutant* of I/JG 2 who had been involved in the 30th of September 1940 combats mentioned in an earlier chapter, found himself flying with his Geschwader Kommodore's *Stabschwarm.* Helmut Wick, the former *Kommandeur* of I/JG 2, had been promoted to *Major* and given command of the whole *Richthofen* Geschwader on the 20th of October 1940 and it was with Wick that Fiby again flew. Flying as wingman to the Geschwader Technical Officer, *Oberleutnant* Rudi Pflanz, Fiby took off with the Geschwader in between 1310 and 1330 hours and headed towards the Isle of Wight. Soon, Helmut Wick began to pull away from the main formation and Pflanz complained that he should slow down. At the head of the whole formation it appeared to Fiby that Wick was keen to improve on his current score of fifty-four 'kills' and ignored Pflanz's pleas. Despite being at least one kilometre ahead, the second pair in the *Schwarm* caught up with Wick just as he attacked a Hurricane and sent it spinning down into the sea north east of the Isle of Wight at 1410 hours. His victim was probably Sergeant Hector Barrow of 213 Squadron whose body was washed ashore in France a few weeks later. The Germans were then bounced by Spitfires of 602 Squadron and a 'dogfight' developed with a further two claims being made by *Oberleutnant* Erich Leie, the Geschwader Adjutant and Wick's wingman, and *Unteroffizier* Gunther Seeger of 3/JG 2. Only one RAF fighter was lost, that being a Spitfire of 602 Squadron flown by Pilot Officer Archibald Lyall who was killed baling out too low, his aircraft crashing near Shanklin on the Isle of Wight. The German formation, low on fuel, then headed back towards the airfield of Querqueville and all had landed by about 1500 hours.

Helmut Wick is interviewed after another victory; far left is Franz Fiby

While this dogfight was taking place, 609 Squadron was in the midst of packing up in preparation for its move to Warmwell. Further chaos ensued when 150 officer cadets from the Sandhurst Military Academy turned up following a rash invitation by Squadron Leader Robinson. As well as the occasional scramble and the packing, these cadets and their instructors were shown what purported to be an orderly and efficient fighter squadron in the morning and followed, surprisingly, by rugby, soccer and hockey matches in the afternoon.

The Squadron did not participate in the combat, which resulted in Helmut Wick's fifty-fifth 'kill' but again, at tea time, was scrambled to intercept a large formation of German aircraft approaching the Isle of Wight. As the Squadron took off, probably witnessed by the Sandhurst cadets, they were not to know that some of their number would not return to finish packing their kit for the move to Warmwell.

At about 1530 hours, Helmut Wick and his Geschwader took off again and headed towards Southampton. It has been suggested that Helmut Wick had been told that his 'rival', *Oberstleutnant* Adolf Galland, *Kommodore* of JG 26, had increased his score of 'kills' earlier that afternoon. Wick, wanting to keep up with Galland, then decided to improve on his score. It was not until the Germans were near the Isle of Wight, that they spotted the fighters of 152 and 609 Squadrons and attacked and Helmut Wick began looking for his fifty-sixth victim.

Keith Ogilvie at the rear of the Squadron caught a glimpse of three yellow noses in his rear view mirror and screamed for the Squadron to break; he managed to dive away but not before he had been hit by cannon

609 taxies out

fire in the rear of his fuselage. Franz Fiby reported attacking two Spitfires and continues:

> They made us work hard – they dived hard and steeply and we gave up the attack. As we were cruising around looking for the rest of the Geschwader, fifteen Spitfires pounced on us from above. I saw one lock on to *Oberleutnant* Pflanz and I yelled 'Rudi! Aircraft above to the left! We must get out of here!' At the same time, my canopy became loose and I broke away. I lost Rudi and flew back home to Querqueville. We still had radio contact and assured each other that we were both okay.
>
> When I was approximately in the centre of the Channel, I heard another aircraft of our Geschwader talking to the Air Sea Rescue service. A pilot had baled out and his parachute was reported fifty kms south-west of the Isle of Wight. I thought I recognised *Major* Wick's voice but later realised it was Rudi Pflanz.

According to *Leutnant* Julius Meimberg of 4/JG 2 who was flying directly behind the *Stabschwarm*, he saw Wick pull away again and at 1613 hours, shot down a Spitfire. His fifty-sixth victim was almost definitely 609's Pilot Officer Paul Baillon who coincidentally had been shot down exactly one month and one day before. Keith Ogilvie, now free from his attackers, saw Baillon bale out twenty miles south of Bournemouth and although Paul's parachute opened and he landed safely in the water, Ogilvie saw no signs of life.

Lt *Julius Meimberg of 4/JG 2*

Pilot Officer Paul Baillon

It would now seem that Wick had become overconfident and, separated from his wingman and Geschwader, became the victim of a lone Spitfire. This was witnessed by *Oberleutnant* Rudi Pflanz who reported:

> After I had lost Fiby, I went low and turned for home. I saw two aircraft in front of me which I flew towards. Too late I recognised the second as a Spitfire. It shot down the Messerschmitt Bf 109 and the pilot baled out. I then shot the Spitfire down; the pilot came down in the sea. I then began talking to the rescue services.

At the height of the air battle, both the RAF controller and Squadron Leader Robinson heard Flight Lieutenant John Dundas say over the radio: 'I've finished an Me 109, Whoopee!' to which Robinson replied: 'Good show John!' after which nothing more was ever seen or heard from John Dundas.

As the Germans began getting low on fuel and ammunition, they broke away for France and safety. Only one German fighter failed to return, that of the *Geschwaderkommodore*. However, for the RAF it was a different matter. In addition to the two lost by 609 Squadron, Sergeant Zygmunt Klein of 152 Squadron was missing whilst Pilot Officer Arthur Watson of the same Squadron was killed when his parachute failed to open after baling out of his burning Spitfire; two aircraft from 609 Squadron were also damaged. The Germans had claimed a further four Spitfires in addition to those shot

Helmut Wick's Messerschmitt Bf 109

down by Wick and Pflanz but the only one that can be matched up is the kill of *Leutnant* Meimberg who reported shooting down a Spitfire in flames, its pilot failing to bale out, his victim almost certainly being Sergeant Klein. The only claim on the RAF side was that for Pilot Officer Eric Marrs of 152 Squadron but this cannot be substantiated unless he damaged Wick and then saw Wick being shot down by Dundas.

The Luftwaffe were shocked by their loss and almost immediately, searches began for Wick's body. These searches continued the next day and were responsible for the high number of scrambles for 609 and other 10 Group Squadrons and were also responsible for delaying 609's departure for Warmwell. However, if the Germans were shocked, so was 609 Squadron by their losses, especially that of John Dundas. The Diary recorded the following tribute:

> Flight Lieutenant John Charles Dundas, the last of the 'A' officers to leave the Squadron, joined it at Yeadon in May 1938 and was one of the more brilliant of the younger journalists of the *Yorkshire Post* and specialized in European international affairs after taking a First in Modern Greats which followed from a modern history examination at Christ Church College, Oxford from Stowe. From the 31st of May to the 28th of November 1940, he accounted for a total of thirteen and a half enemy aircraft destroyed, seven enemy aircraft damaged and four probable. His courageous example and breezy personality are sorely missed.

As for Paul Baillon:

> He had only recently joined the Squadron and had but little opportunity of dropping his card on the Luftwaffe. A typical Norman in appearance, a solicitor by profession, quiet, unassuming, competent and not without personal charm, his loss is deplored by all his comrades. He leaves a widow who was about to present him with an offspring.

The loss experienced by the Squadron must have been great. Not only had it lost two pilots but also one of its most popular and successful. Added to that, some might think that John Dundas' death meant that the auxiliary connection died with him. True in the case of the pilots now left on the Squadron but many of its groundcrew were auxiliaries before the war, and regarded themselves as auxiliaries then and still regard themselves as auxiliaries today.

The misery must have been compounded in the weeks that followed. Warmwell was not much better, according to the Operations Record Book writer, than when they were there back in August 1940. The airmen apparently preferred Warmwell because of better food but the pilots were still 'not amused'. Coupled with the vagaries of winter and the month of December being 'almost entirely a barren month from an operational viewpoint', one can guess how the Squadron probably felt.

The only conclusive combat for the month occurred on the 2nd of December when Pilot Officer Noel Agazarian and Flying Officer 'Novi' Nowierski claimed a Messerschmitt Bf 110 south of Thorney Island, the Coastal Command airfield near to Chichester. Having 'given it the works', their victim apparently plunged into the Channel but not before being

claimed by anti-aircraft fire (which almost claimed Noel Agazarian as well). Despite this, the identify of their victim is not known. Only on three more occasions during the month did the Squadron see the Luftwaffe and in each combat the Germans managed to escape without damage.

Despite the few combats in the air, battles were being fought on the ground against the elements and the airfield, not the Luftwaffe. As the sun rose on the 6th of December, the Squadron found that its dispersal had been flattened by gales experienced during the night. The operations marquee and most of the other tents were down and telephone lines washed away. However, by the afternoon, the tents were up and the telephone lines discovered and reconnected. Annoyingly, eight days later, the elements struck again. As Flight Sergeant Cloves recorded:

> Another gale hit us during the morning of the 14th of December and once more, the operations tent 'went for a burton'; a downpour of rain added to the fun. The operations blokes and three pilots extricated themselves from the wreckage and salvage operations commenced. The whole moved *en bloc* to the airmen's marquee, the GPO were summoned to move the telephones and life went on as usual. We fight the Jerries and the elements!

It was left to the Operations Record Book to set the final scene for 1940:

At the time of writing, the shelter at dispersal point still consisted of a few unstable canvas erections surrounded by a swamp. As the newspaper say 'A Happy New year to all Our Readers.

So came to an end 609's second year of the war and for the purpose of this book, 609's story.* The Squadron had experienced a far more tumultuous year than the previous one as twelve months before, they had failed to even shoot down a single German aircraft but at the same time, had not lost any pilots. The same could not have been said of the Luftwaffe. They had experienced Poland, Denmark and Norway, the invasion of France and the Low Countries before the Battle of Britain and it was a far more experienced Luftwaffe, in comparison to the RAF, that had commenced *Phase One* of the attack on Great Britain back in July 1940. However, after reading 609's account of the Battle of Britain, one might think that it was a battered, broken and beaten Luftwaffe that lay on the other side of the Channel, having claimed few RAF victims but having lost so much more. The chapters that now follow tell the story of another squadron's Battle of Britain but this time it is the story of a squadron flying different aircraft with different markings, the pilots speaking a different language and flying from French airfields.

---

* *The Story of 609 Squadron: Under the White Rose* by Frank Ziegler published by *Crécy Books*, 1993, documents the full and exciting history of this Squadron – *Author*

CHAPTER SEVEN

Prelude to the Battle (2)

The Treaty of Versailles which followed Germany's defeat in the First World War aimed to curtail Germany's economic power and emasculate its armed forces. The Air Clauses of this Treaty were designed to end German military aviation and under the supervision of the Allied Control Commission, the German Flying Corps surrendered all of its aeronautical equipment to the victorious allies.

However, what the Allies failed to take into consideration was German civil aviation. There were some limitations as to the size of civil aircraft that Germany could build but the Paris Air Agreement of 1926 effectively withdrew these restrictions. Thus, Germany bean expanding commercial aviation at an unprecedented rate with the establishment of airlines, flying clubs and aviation training schools. Germany's aircraft industry also began to pick up the pace so that when the German Chancellor Adolf Hitler and his Nazi party seized control of Germany in 1933, the rate of expansion of Germany's civil as well as military aviation was easily increased. The birth of the *Pik As Geschwader* was soon to follow.

On the 1st of April 1937, JG 334 came into existence with its *Geschwaderstab* and *I Gruppe* based at Wiesbaden-Erbenheim and *II Gruppe* based at Mannheim-Sandhofen. The whole Geschwader was equipped with the Arado Ar 68 biplane fighter. Over the next year, the Geschwader continued to train and expand, converting to the brand new Messerschmitt Bf 109B monoplane. 1938 also saw pilots from JG 334 joining *Jagdgruppe J/88* and participating in the Spanish Civil War as part of the German Condor Legion. Pilots included *Oberleutnant* Werner Mölders, *Oberleutnant* Hans-Karl Mayer, *Oberfeldwebel* Walter Grimmling, *Oberfeldwebel* Alfred Müller, *Unteroffizier* Alfred Stark and *Unteroffizier* Guenther Freund, all of whom were later to fly with 1/JG 53.

The pace of change began to quicken when in September 1938, JG 334 participated in the German Sudetenland Crisis. The Geschwader was renumbered JG 133 in November and, early in 1939, its Messerschmitt Bf 109Ds were replaced by the latest model of Messerschmitt Bf 109, the E version. Soon to become universally known throughout the Luftwaffe as the 'Emil' it remained with the Geschwader for over the next two tumultuous years.

In May 1939 JG 133 was renumbered JG 53 and, accordingly, the *Staffeln* were also renumbered. It was at this time that *1 Staffel/Jagdgeschwader 53* was born. 1/JG 53 was fortunate from the start with its first *Staffelkapitän*

I/JG 53, April 1938. Oberleutnant *Werner Mölders is seventh from the right, to his left is* Leutnant *Hans-Karl Mayer*

Ofw *Walter Grimmling*

Uffz *Bezner is awarded the Iron Cross for his first kill*

being none other than the holder of the Spanish Cross in Gold with swords
and diamonds – *Hauptmann* Werner Mölders. Having returned from Spain
with fourteen confirmed 'kills', his experience and the tactical awareness
gained in Spain would benefit his Staffel, as well as the Luftwaffe, when
war broke out later that year. Even his deputy *Staffelkapitän*, *Oberleutnant*
Hans-Karl Mayer, had gained eight 'kills' in Spain and was the holder of
the Spanish Cross in Gold with Swords.

As 1939 progressed, the politicians began to fail in their efforts to avoid
all-out War. When German troops invaded Poland on the 1st of September
1939, it was only two more days before Britain and France declared war
on Germany. The Second World War had begun.

On the Western Front, Britain, France and Germany did not immediately experience the full horrors of war. From September 1939 to May
1940, the enemies faced each other in what became known as the 'Phoney
War' (or in German the *Sitzkrieg* or 'sitting war'). Unlike 609 Squadron, who
had to wait five months for their first kill, 1/JG 53 scored its and,
incidentally, the Geschwader's first victory six days after the start of the war
in the west. The credit was given to former Condor Legion pilot
Oberfeldwebel Walter Grimmling who on the morning of the 9th of
September 1939 shot down a French Air Force Bloch 131 of *Groupe Aerien
de Reconnaissance I/14* which crashed north-east of Saarbrücken in Germany
killing its pilot *Sergeant Chef* Bouvry and gunner with a third crew member
being wounded. The following day, Grimmling and his wing man
Unteroffizier Heinrich Bezner claimed two Mureaux 115s. Both pilots were
awarded the Iron Cross Second Class for these victories and the first such
awards for the whole Geschwader.

As Summer became Autumn, the kills for the Staffel increased but at a
slower rate. *Hauptmann* Mölders shot down his first victim of the war, a
Curtiss H-75A of *Groupe de Chasse II/5*, on the 20th of September; it was
to be his first and last kill whilst with 1/JG 53 as ten days later, he was posted
to be *Kommandeur* of II/JG 53. His place as *Staffelkapitän* was taken by his
deputy *Oberleutnant* Hans-Karl Mayer who had to wait a further month for
his first kill of the war when he shot down a Potez 637 of *Group Aerien de
Reconnaissance II/33* near Saarburg in Germany on the 5th of November.
This was to be the last victory for the Staffel for nearly five and a half
months.

During these first few months of the war, *1 Staffel* did not escape without
casualties. Their first loss occurred on the 12th of November when *Feldwebel*
Günther Bleidorn was shot down and killed over German territory near
Sanddorf. Even 1940 started badly when on the 2nd of January 1940, the
Staffel came off worse in a combat with sixteen Curtiss H-75s with *Leutnant*
Hans Ohly (who was on his second operational flight having joined the
Staffel only two weeks previously) being wounded after crash landing his
damaged fighter near Birkenfeld in Germany and *Leutnant* Walter Rupp's
Messerschmitt Bf 109 being damaged by gunfire.

The pace of the war must now seemed to have dragged to all the *1 Staffel*
pilots as the other *Staffeln* and *Gruppen* were having the occasional success
but not them. Activity was further curtailed by the severe winter and the

The first loss – Fw Günther Bleidorn

Fw *Bleidorn's grave*

arrival of spring must have been welcomed. However, the air war for *1 Staffel* began again in earnest on the 21st of April 1940 when on a *Freie Jagd* fighter sweep over German territory in the Trier-Pirmasens area, Hans-Karl Mayer spotted two enemy fighters and on approaching unseen from behind, shot one of them down near Merzig. This was the first meeting of *1 Staffel*, in combat, with the RAF and one of its newest fighters, the Hawker Hurricane, even if the battle was very one sided. The Hurricane pilot, Flying Officer Peter Walker of 73 Squadron, was lucky and suffered only slight wounds from Hans-Karl Mayer's attack. Walker managed to bale out and landed near Königsmacker in France.

On the 10th of May 1940 the Phoney War ended when the Germans started their offensive in the West. *Leutnant* Hans Ohly who had been wounded on the 2nd of January had only returned to flying duties a week earlier, his wounds healed. He flew his first operational flight on the 12th of May and managed to get three more flights in before the Staffel's first mission on the 14th. The day was relatively quiet until the Staffel's third mission when they then met the RAF again. In the space of twenty-two minutes, six *1 Staffel* pilots claimed two Hurricanes, six Fairey Battles and six Bristol Blenheims near the French town of Sedan. The Staffel lost two pilots and three fighters – *Oberfeldwebel* Walter Grimmling was shot down in combat with a Hurricane, his fighter and body later being found near Bouillon while *Feldwebel* Alfred Stark made the mistake of getting too close to the Blenheim that he had attacked and set on fire; the Blenheim exploded taking the German fighter and its pilot with it. The only pilot to return was *Unteroffizier* Herbert Tzschoppe who had managed to crash-land his fighter in German held territory near Sedan.

Hurricanes of 73 Squadron

Opposite above
73 Squadron's first casualties – Flying Officer Peter Walker is far left

Opposite below
1 Staffel *takes a rest, June 1940. Left to right:* Lt *Zeis,* Uffz *Höhnisch,* Oblt *Mayer,* Lt *Schultz,* Uffz *Tzschoppe,* Fw *Bezner*

Oblt *Hans Ohly*

Scenes at Rennes – French soldiers help rebuld the airfield whilst the remains of French aircraft lie around

The Staffel was not able to repeat their success of the 14th of May only scoring a further four victories up to the 9th of June 1940. By that time, they had moved from their base in Germany to fly from the former French Air Force airfields of Sedan-Douzy, Charleville and, from the 23rd of June, Rennes. In the latter stages of the French Campaign the Staffel only lost a further three fighters with one pilot wounded and two prisoners of the French.* The number of missions now began to reduce as the German military machine, having reached the Channel coast, achieved its objective. The Staffel now began to fly closer to England when on the 8th of July, they flew over Guernsey while settling in to their new home at Rennes. Time was mainly spent resting and recovering with pilots soon seeing the sights of Paris.

All now knew that the next task for the Staffel would be in connection with the invasion of England. Despite the successes of the 14th of May, the Staffel only met the RAF on one other occasion in the weeks that followed when *Oberfeldwebel* Alfred Müller shot down a 150 Squadron Fairey Battle north east of Sedan. With the RAF fighters operating from their home bases, the Staffel having to fly at the limit of their 'Emil's' endurance and having to fly and fight over the sea, many must have wondered what the weeks that followed would bring. The first flight over England was scheduled for the 2nd of August but was cancelled due to bad weather. To make matters worse, the next two missions on the 8th and 9th of August were also cancelled. As the Staffel flew from Rennes to their advance airfield at Cherbourg-East on the morning of the 11th of August, many of its pilots must have wondered if this time they were going to get the chance to write in their logbooks 'First Mission against England!'. For 1/JG 53, the Battle of Britain was about to start.

* Both of the captured pilots were liberated by German forces and returned to flying duties
– *Author*

CHAPTER EIGHT

If I am Shot Down, Keep my Pistol

1/JG 53's first *Englandeinsatz* (literally 'operation against England') came on Sunday the 11th of August 1940. Having flown from Rennes to Cherbourg-East, the Staffel took off on an escort mission at 1000 hours and landed an hour and twenty minutes later without any victories. Relief must have been great at getting the first *Englandeinsatz* over and without loss but they must have felt jealous at the successes of the rest of the Geschwader as *II Gruppe* claimed one and *III Gruppe* claimed five RAF fighters destroyed. *I Gruppe* victories were claimed by *Oberleutnant* Rudolf Schmid of *2 Staffel* and *Leutnant* Siegfried Fischer of *3 Staffel** although these kills cannot be confirmed. The days that followed would be different for *1 Staffel*.

At about 0905 hours on the 12th of August, the Staffel took off from Rennes on a sweep of the French Coast with the orders to look for anything out of the ordinary and having seen nothing of note, landed at Cherbourg-East forty minutes later. Shortly afterwards, the Gruppe was briefed as to their next mission which was to escort the Junkers Ju 88s of KG 51 for an attack on Portsmouth Harbour and the radar station at Ventnor on the Isle of Wight. Taking off at 1030 hours, *1 Staffel* headed off to start their fighter sweep in and around the Isle of Wight but after about thirty minutes, *Oberleutnant* Hans Ohly reported that he was suffering from problems with his Messerschmitt's throttle and engine acceleration. Hans Ohly headed back for Cherbourg-East and landed, without incident, at 1230 hours not knowing that as he was approaching the French Coast, his Staffel were involved in a very one sided air battle.

At 1220 hours, *Hauptmann* Hans-Karl Mayer spotted three Hurricanes attacking a damaged Messerschmitt Bf 110. Before he could get in a position to attack, the Hurricanes succeeded in setting the defenceless twin-engined fighter on fire and Mayer saw the German pilot bale out; immediately afterwards, *1 Staffel* bounced the unsuspecting RAF fighters. Mayer opened fire from forty metres closing to thirty metres and poured twenty 20mm rounds and eighty 7.92mm rounds into the right hand Hurricane. The RAF pilot did not have a chance as his fighter burst into flames and plunged into the Channel at 1222 hours; Mayer later reported that the pilot must have been dead before his fighter hit the water. At exactly the same time Mayer's wing man, *Unteroffizier* Heinrich Rühl attacked the left hand Hurricane at a range of one hundred metres closing

---

* *Leutnant* Fischer transferred to *1 Staffel* in September 1940 – *Author*

to fifty metres. Heinrich Rühl's fighter was a Messerschmitt Bf.109E-1, this variant of 'Emil' not being armed with the 20mm cannon and as a result, he needed to fire two hundred rounds of 7.92mm at his quarry which tried desperately to get away from him but to no avail as this Hurricane also plunged into the Channel taking its pilot with it.

The final Hurricane of the doomed RAF section now received the undivided attention of Hans-Karl Mayer. This combat was not so one-sided as the RAF pilot had managed to damage Mayer's fighter in the tail before Mayer fatally damaged his aircraft. He then attempted to head for the safety of the Hampshire Coast but Mayer noted dense black smoke emitting from the Hurricane and shortly afterwards it hit the water in a shallow dive and sank. Again, there was no sign of the RAF pilot.

Many Hurricanes were lost this day making it hard to ascertain for certain who were the victims of Mayer and Rühl. However, it is possible that the *1 Staffel* pilots were responsible for shooting down Pilot Officer John Harrison and the two Polish pilots Flight Lieutenant Wilhelm Pankratz and Sergeant Josef Kwiecinski. These three Hurricane pilots from 145 Squadron were shot down off the Isle of Wight at about 1230 hours and are to this day still reported as missing.

At the same time as Mayer and Rühl were shooting down 1/JG 53's first victims of the Battle of Britain, another pilot from the Staffel was shooting down his first aircraft of the war. *Unteroffizier* Heinrich Kopperschläger was a popular pilot within the Staffel; tall and with a hearty appetite, one of his tricks in the air was to hide himself from the view of his wing man giving the impression that nobody was flying his Messerschmitt. However, today he was in a more serious frame of mind, flying with *Unteroffizier* Heinrich Höhnisch as the *Deckungsschwarm* (literally 'protection Schwarm' – their job being to protect the rest of the Staffel from being attacked from above). As *1 Staffel* commenced their attack on the Hurricanes, Kopperschläger and Höhnisch scanned the skies for danger. Heinrich Kopperschläger reported what happened next as follows:

> The Staffel attacked three Hurricanes but I was flying in the *Deckungsschwarm*. After I saw *Hauptmann* Mayer shoot down a Hurricane, I noticed behind the Staffel a single machine. As I turned towards it, I saw that it was a Spitfire. He attempted to break away to escape. He then tried to dive away. At forty metres, I opened fire at him. He attempted to break away to the left but suddenly, I saw a white fuel trail and he crashed into the water. The pilot did not bale out.

The RAF lost three Spitfires off the Isle of Wight that lunch time with two pilots reported missing and the third pilot's body being found in the Channel almost a month later. A further Spitfire crashed on the Isle of Wight, its pilot managing to run away from his fighter before it exploded.

A jubilant *1 Staffel* returned to Cherbourg-East, elated at its successes and not having suffered any casualties. Only the Staffel leader's aircraft was damaged and he was photographed later that day at Cherbourg-East sitting astride his damaged fighter – a small price to pay for such successes. The rest of the Geschwader managed to shoot down a further four fighters but

Heinrich Höhnisch and Heinrich Kopperschläger

suffered the loss of *Hauptmann* Harro Harder, the experienced *Gruppenkommandeur* of III/JG 53 and former Condor Legion pilot. After claiming two Spitfires, he himself had been shot down, his body being washed ashore at Dieppe one month and one day later. Unusually, later that afternoon the temporary *Kommandeur* of III/JG 53, *Hauptmann* Wolf-Dietrich Wilcke, almost became the second *Kommandeur* of III/JG 53 to be lost in one day when his fighter suffered an engine failure whilst on an escort mission for German search and rescue seaplanes. He baled out and thanks to the moonlight, was lucky to be spotted in the sea later that night by a member of his Staffel and was soon picked up by a German seaplane.

Hans-Karl Mayer sits by the damage done to his fighter, 13 August 1940

1 Staffel did not return to Rennes that evening, presumably remaining at Cherbourg-East overnight in preparation for *Adlertag* which was scheduled for the following day. On the 13th of August 1940 the Staffel took off at 0605 hours for an escort mission for the Junkers Ju 88's of KG 54, landing seventy minutes later without incident. Their fighters refuelled and rearmed and the pilots fed and rested, they took off again at 1530 hours and again headed for England. The task of I/JG 53 was to fly a fighter sweep in the Portland/Weymouth area whilst *II Gruppe*, who had taken off from Guernsey ten minutes before *I Gruppe*, had the onerous task of escorting the Stukas of II/StG 2. *1 Staffel* again picked on their favourite prey, Hurricanes, and claimed to have shot down four off Portland. However, RAF losses are harder to match this time as although a number of fighters managed to return damaged, as illustrated by 609 Squadron's two casualties, one being a Spitfire returning to base with bullet holes in the fuselage and another returning with its fuel and oil lines severed by gunfire, only two RAF fighters crashed in the Channel. One was the Hurricane of Sergeant Philip Norris of 213 Squadron whose body was later washed ashore in France, the other was the Hurricane flown by Sergeant Henry Marsh of 238 Squadron which failed to return from a combat in the Portland area. A further loss was Sergeant Ronald Little of 238 Squadron whose Hurricane crashed at Burton Bradstock, Dorset, but Little survived the crash unhurt. Nonetheless, the four claims by *1 Staffel* were

An earlier accident suffered by Sergeant Marsh of 238 Squadron – Hurricane P2946 on 19 July 40

Uffz Werner Karl *returns from a mission in his 'White 14', August 1940*

accepted, as were a further four claims by II/JG 53 (a further claim by *II Gruppe* not being accepted).

By now *1 Staffel* had claimed thirty-six confirmed victories out of the ninety-eight claimed by the whole Gruppe. Confidence was running high with the German pilots but all were aware that sooner or later they would suffer casualties. So far only two fighters had been slightly damaged which was a very small price to pay for eight confirmed victories. Still, this did not prevent the German pilots from talking about what could happen to them. The 'baby' of the Staffel was twenty-year-old *Unteroffizier* Werner Karl who had arrived in June 1940 as a replacement for one of the pilots shot down in the previous month. He remembers what he felt at that time about the possibility of being shot down:

> There was no talk about fear or of being killed or taken prisoner. At least, nobody admitted if he was scared. All around us, we saw heroes both in the newspapers and on the radio. I think that everybody thought that he was the only one who was afraid. For instance, when the briefing finished for the next mission, we all ran to the latrines. At first we thought it was sabotage but in fact it was fear.

Most of the Staffel, although issued with a Walther PPK pistol, refused to fly with them. Another pilot, *Unteroffizier* Willi Ghesla (pronounced 'Gayzler') had moved from *2 Staffel* in June 1940, again to bring the Staffel back to full strength following the loss of a number of *1 Staffel* pilots.

Uffz *Willi Ghesla sits on the wing of his 'Emil', Rennes, August 1940*

1 Staffel *pilots, Rennes, August 1940. Left to right: Ghesla, Tzschoppe, Höhnisch, Zeis, Ohly, Mayer, Schultz, Karl and Rühl*

He remembers:

> Four of us, Herbert Tzschoppe, Werner Karl, Heinrich Höhnisch and myself, left our pistols in our accommodation as we felt they were useless if we were ever shot down. We had this mutual agreement and would say: 'If I am shot down keep my pistol'. I was not to know that within a month, I would have a total of four.

The day after *Adlertag* was an anti-climax; due to the bad weather, only the occasional flight along the French Coast was flown. However, the following day saw the Staffel breaking with the normal pattern as on Thursday the 15th of August, they had a few extra hours in bed before taking off for their advance airfield at 1400 hours. Their mission this day was escort for the attacks by I and II/LG 1 against the airfields of Middle Wallop and Worthy Down. Taking off at 1650 hours, the Staffel took great delight in shooting down six barrage balloons, a fact noted with alarm by the Winchester Royal Observer Corps post who thought that the balloons were aircraft crashing in flames. Shortly afterwards, Hans-Karl Mayer scored the only victory for the Staffel when he spotted a Hurricane attacking a Messerschmitt Bf 110. He dived, gave the Hurricane three short bursts of fire and saw it roll over and crash near Salisbury at 1746 hours. The only possible RAF victim was Pilot Officer Gordon Cleaver of 601 Squadron whose Hurricane crashed near Winchester at approximately 1745 hours. Gordon Cleaver baled out wounded and never again flew operationally.

Hans-Karl Mayer's 'Emil' showing his kills up to 15 August 1940

The Staffel returned to Cherbourg-East and on getting out of their fighters, headed off to their tent for a debrief. All of them were to receive a nasty shock, as Werner Karl remembers:

Richard Hardy's Spitfire after landing at Cherbourg-East, 15 August 1940

> Somebody shouted: 'Spitfire!' and I looked up to see a Spitfire coming over the airfield. Anti-aircraft guns opened fire and the Spitfire banked around and landed. Having got over the shock, we crowded around the Spitfire. The pilot got out and surrendered to *Hauptmann* Rolf Pingel, Staffelkapitän of 2/JG 53.

Pilot Officer Richard Hardy of 234 Squadron had been in action off the Isle of Wight and how he came to be over Cherbourg is open to much conjecture. However, he was slightly wounded in the back, either by cannon fire or when his Identification Friend or Foe transmitter was detonated. After first aid, he was entertained by the pilots of *I Gruppe* in the Pilot's Mess before being taken off to a Prisoner of War Camp. His aircraft remained a considerable source of interest to JG 53's pilots as well as the other German pilots that used the airfield.

The following day, the 16th of August, the Staffel flew two escort sorties, one taking off at 1230 hours, the second at 1620 hours. Although the Staffel engaged RAF fighters in a series of vicious combats, no claims were submitted. It was probably on this day that *Unteroffizier* Werner Karl recorded his first and only kill:

> We had returned to Cherbourg-East from a mission over England to refuel before heading back to Rennes. I was the last to be refuelled and by the time my fighter was ready, the rest of the Staffel had already taken off. I took off alone and set course for Rennes. It was quite cloudy but near Mont St Michel on the northern French Coast I broke out of cloud to see in front of me a Spitfire. I could not believe it and in my excitement fired my first burst well out of range. However, my second burst hit the Spitfire and it plunged into

Uffz Karl dozes by his 'White 14'

the sea. I landed at Rennes full of excitement and the Staffel took off to try and find evidence of my success. However, nothing was found and my claim was not allowed.

No mention of this combat can be found in any surviving documents but on the evening of the 16th of August, *Oberleutnant* Hans Ohly recorded taking off on a sweep along the French Coast an hour after landing back at Rennes and it is assumed that searching for Werner Karl's victim could have been the intention for this flight.

The 17th of August was a day of rest for the Staffel but the day after they were back in action again. The mission was to escort Stukas in their attacks on airfields at Thorney Island and Tangmere in Sussex. For *Oberleutnant* Hans Ohly the day was not a success as, after taking off at 1208 hours for Cherbourg-East, his personal Messerschmitt Bf 109E-4, coded 'White 7', suffered engine problems and he was forced to land at Montbourg. His fighter was soon repaired and an hour and a half later, he took off for Cherbourg-East. Refuelled and briefed, ninety minutes after landing he took off with the Staffel on the escort sortie only to suffer undercarriage problems which forced him to abort the mission. However, the Staffel did manage to shoot down three RAF fighters without loss but details of what exactly happened are not known – the combat reports for this day no longer exist and unusually, Hans Ohly made no mention of the Staffel successes in his logbook, probably because of his extreme annoyance at not having participated in the battles.

Oblt *Ohly's 'White 7'*

1 Staffel *at St Malo on one of their rare days off. Willi Ghesla and Werner Karl look out towards England*

As well as no record of the 18th of August combats, information on what happened to the Staffel in the days leading up to the 24th of August is scant. On the 19th of August, Hans Ohly took his 'White 7' on a test flight only to have the same undercarriage problem manifest itself again. The Staffel flew to its advance airfield on the 20th of August, to find the intended mission scrubbed because of bad weather, the same happening three days later. However, the Staffel did apparently fly on the 22nd of August and is reputed to have claimed to have shot down two RAF aircraft – again no documentary evidence, German or British, has survived to prove or disprove these victories.

These days of inactivity must have been welcomed by the Staffel who had been in constant action for just over a week. With no flying planned, the Staffel would go *en masse* to nearby restaurants in Rennes normally chosen by Hans-Karl Mayer for their fine cuisine. Letter writing, visits to the coast, playing cards or just talking helped take their minds off the War but for some, unusual tasks had to be undertaken, as Werner Karl recalls:

I remember being ordered to fly to Guernsey and load up my fighter with as many tomatoes as it could carry. It was a chance to get in some extra flying but I did not like tomatoes so was not interested in my cargo. On my return to Rennes I remember telling *Oberleutnant* Ohly of my dislike of tomatoes and he promised to cook them in such a way that I would change my mind. I still said no when the tomatoes were put in front of me and I was almost ordered to eat them. However, *Oberleutnant* Ohly was right and I have eaten and enjoyed tomatoes from that day to this!

Some pilots took advantage of flying the Staffel's war booty – a captured Potez 63 twin engined French bomber but it wasn't long before most of the pilots who flew this plane began to treat their 'toy' with great mistrust, not helped by the fact that its previous owner's unit badge was a skeleton carrying a scythe! *Unteroffizier* Heinrich Höhnisch remembered the dangerous swing when the throttles were opened on take-off and its unpleasant flying characteristics. Soon no one would fly the death trap! However, the Staffel would not have either the time or opportunity for pleasure flying in the days and weeks that followed.

The war restarted for the Staffel on the 24th and 25th of August, and an account of what occurred has been detailed in Chapters One and Two. Unfortunately, the Staffel's luck had at last broken on the 25th of August with its first loss of the Battle of Britain; from now on, the losses would start to increase.

The next mission, the last to be flown from Rennes and Cherbourg-East, was another escort mission this time for the Heinkel He 111s of KG 55 which were briefed to attack Portsmouth. JG 53, together with JG 2 and JG 27, took off at about 1550 hours and, in a similar fashion to the previous two days, the massive formation headed towards the Isle of Wight. 1 Staffel's task was a *Freie Jagd* in the Portsmouth/Selsey Bill area and as usual it was not long before Hans-Karl Mayer spotted enemy fighters. At 1630 hours, when twenty kms east of Portsmouth, he saw five Hurricanes heading towards the Heinkels. Singling out one, he fired a mere twelve rounds of 20mm ammunition and thirty 7.92mm rounds into a Hurricane

The death trap – a Potez 63 of 1 Staffel

which immediately caught fire and dived away into cloud. Hans-Karl Mayer concluded that the Hurricane pilot was both young and inexperienced to allow him such an easy victory. Five minutes later, he spotted what was to be his nineteenth victory. Intent on shooting down one of the attacking Heinkels, Sergeant Cyril Babbage of 602 Squadron committed the basic error of not looking behind him. If he had, he would have seen *Hauptmann* Mayer, with his *Rottenflieger*, *Unteroffizier* Werner Karl, close behind almost sitting on his tail. Mayer again used few rounds to bring down Babbage's Spitfire which caught fire and dived away. All of this was observed by *Leutnant* Julius Haase, Adjutant of I/JG 53 who, flying a thousand metres higher than *1 Staffel*, saw the unequal battle between a Messerschmitt Bf 109 coded 'White 8' and a Spitfire whose pilot baled out and landed in the sea. Cyril Babbage was rescued by life boat and safely landed at Selsey, more worried about the damage that the sea water had done to the pound notes in his wallet than what could well have been his demise.

Richard Gayner (left, seen with Flight Lieutenant Trevor Williams). Photo taken in 1943 when Richard Gayner was flying with 68 Squadron

Meanwhile, the final air battle of the day was being fought between *Leutnant* Alfred Zeis and what he identified as a Spitfire. Instructed to fly in the *Deckungsschwarm*, he attacked the right hand of two fighters north-east of Portsmouth and saw it catch fire and dive away into the cloud. His victim is not known but Flying Officer Richard Gayner of 615 Squadron whose Hurricane was bounced and shot down in the same area at the same time, gives a vivid account of being one of the Luftwaffe's seven victims and one of the RAF's seven casualties in this afternoon air battle:

> That morning we had scrambled to go after a balbo which I believe was attacking Debden and Hornchurch. I probably got a squirt at a Heinkel 111. When we scrambled from Kenley to go after the Portsmouth attack, the air seemed full of huns. At what height, I do not know, but I am inclined to think that it was more than 10,000 feet.
>
> I was flying from the north west towards the Heinkels and should think that we were about 1,000 feet higher than they were. I do not remember where the rest of the Squadron was but wham! He got me. As usual, I did not see him.
>
> I crash-landed on Charlton Down near to Horndean, in a mess, wheels up and covered in barbed wire (presumably erected there to deter airborne landing). I was covered in glycol as well as oil. I think that I had to side slip from side to side to get a forward view through the stream of glycol. I was bleeding from the mouth and feared an internal injury but this turned out to be merely my bitten or cut tongue. My wife said that I also had a bit of armour plate in me from a cannon shell. I have no memory of whether I managed to get out myself or whether people came and lifted me out of the cockpit.

1 Staffel pay their last respects at the grave of Fw *Bezner. Left to right: Fischer, Mayer, Schultz, Ohly and* Zeis

1 Staffel headed back for Cherbourg-East but for the second day in succession they left one of their number behind but this time it was not the RAF that had accounted for the German casualty. *Feldwebel* Heinrich Bezner's fighter suffered an engine failure and was seen to dive into the sea south of Portsmouth; no sign of him was seen until nearly a month later when his body was washed ashore at Boulogne, ironically not too far from where his Staffel was then flying. It was Heinrich Bezner that had scored one of the Staffel's first kills nearly a year previously. Luck had evaded him since then and at the time of his death, he had still that one victory to his name. He was buried with full military honours near Boulogne at the end of September, his Staffel in attendance.

Two days later, *1 Staffel* moved from Rennes to Montreuil-Neuville in the Pas de Calais in preparation for the next phase of the Battle of Britain, the aerial assault against London. Their actions so far in the Battle of Britain had been rewarded with 26 victories in the space of sixteen days at the cost of one pilot killed and one Prisoner of War. The Staffel however was soon to find the pace of war increase and they would not be able to repeat these initial successes and light losses for the remainder of the Battle of Britain.

CHAPTER NINE

You Should be Happy being in Captivity!

The move to the Pas de Calais occurred without incident and the pilots found themselves billeted in a pleasant hotel near the beach at Le Touquet. *I Gruppe* would operate out of the airfield at Montreuil-Neuville, *II Gruppe* out of Sempy and *III Gruppe* would be operating out of Le Touquet. As well as a change of airfields, a number of changes also occurred to both aircraft and personnel.

Because of the vast numbers of German fighters operating out of airfields in the Pas de Calais area identification in the air became paramount. As a result, the noses, cowlings, wing tips and rudders of the Messerschmitt Bf 109s were roughly painted with either yellow or white paint. JG 53, who for some obscure reason had been forbidden to fly with their 'Ace of Spades' badge earlier during the month and in defiance had painted red rings around their Messerschmitt's cowlings, now painted red rings over

An 'Emil' of 2/JG 53 is pushed back into its dispersal, clearly showing the yellow/white tactical markings on the nose and red band under the exhaust stubs

the yellow or white paint giving their fighters a most gaudy appearance. On the personnel side the *Staffelkapitän* of *2 Staffel*, *Hauptmann* Rolf Pingel, had been posted to command I/JG 26 and was replaced from within the Staffel by the experienced *Oberleutnant* Ignatz Prestelle. *Hauptmann* Wolfgang Lippert, *Staffelkapitän* of 3/JG 53, was posted to command II/JG 27 and was replaced by *Oberleutnant* Julius Haase. The last posting was that of *Hauptmann* Hans-Karl Mayer. Shortly after *1 Staffel* had settled in at Neuville, he was told that he would be succeeding *Major* Albert Blumensaat as the *Kommandeur* of I/JG 53 – a popular choice for the pilots of *I Gruppe* but *1 Staffel* must have been sad to loose their successful leader. However, his successor was chosen from within the Staffel; *Oberleutnant* Hans Ohly would lead the Staffel from the 2nd of September onwards. All three former *Staffelkapitäne* were to be further rewarded for their efforts with the Knight's

Hptm *Mayer after his award of the Knight's Cross*

Hptm *Pingel, former*
Staffelkapitän *of 2/JG*
53, another Knight's
Cross recipient (seen
talking to Hans-Karl
Mayer), between them is
Oblt *Heinz Wittmeyer of*
2/JG 53

Cross. Hans-Karl Mayer, who now had nineteen victory bars on the rudder of his fighter, was awarded the prestigious decoration on the 3rd of September, Rolf Pingel,' with ten victories, on the 14th of September and Wolfgang Lippert, who had eleven by the time he left the Geschwader, on the 24th of September. Hans-Karl Mayer or Mayer-*Ast* as he was called behind his back (*Ast* meaning bough or branch, a joke being made of Mayer's height and size) had a few more missions to fly as *Staffelkapitän* before leaving.

The Staffel's first mission against London was flown the day after their arrival in the Pas de Calais. It was yet another escort mission but the RAF failed to lock horns with JG 53. The day after, the 30th of August, *1 Staffel* took part in covering the return flight of a bomber formation, meeting the German bombers over Dover. The Staffel is said to have claimed three RAF aircraft but positive confirmation is not available. However, one of the pilots said to have claimed a victory was *Unteroffizier* Willi Ghesla. Although he cannot remember exact details of his first 'kill', the following account could well have described it:

> I was on the return from a flight over England. In the distance, I saw a plane so I went straight to it. It was one of our twin-engined bombers. One engine was hit and was out of action so I flew alongside the bomber to protect the crew against further attacks. Shortly, a British fighter appeared and tried to shoot the bomber down. I cannot be sure if I shot down the RAF fighter but I did prevent him from attacking the bomber so I was able to save the German crew and escort them home safely. It was the most satisfactory flight for me for the whole war.

On the 31st of August, JG 53 attacked English barrage balloons for the second time as, during the morning mission it helped shoot down twenty balloons over the Thames Estuary. *Oberleutnant* Hans Ohly was, however, very annoyed that he could not shoot down more because his guns had jammed. In the evening, Dover's balloon barrage was the object of their intention when a further sixteen were shot down by the Staffel. The German pilots enjoyed this 'sport', especially when the RAF fighters did not spoil their enjoyment. *Unteroffizier* Werner Karl remembers the latter mission very well. Having followed his *Staffelkapitän* into the attack, he emerged from the balloon barrage at a very low height and the object of Dover's anti-aircraft gun's intentions. He flew down to sea level and continued along the length of the Dover Mole, clearly remembering the guns firing over his cockpit roof. At full throttle, he sped out towards France as if 'the devil was on his tail', getting back without any damage. In two days time Werner Karl would see Dover again but on this occasion, he would not be flying back to France. At the end of this day's activity *1 Staffel* claimed four RAF aircraft shot down but these were unconfirmed.

Throughout the first day of September the escort missions continued with the Staffel escorting bombers on the first mission of the day, over the Thames Estuary. Although the Staffel was engaged in combat, only *III Gruppe* and the *Kommandeur* of II/JG 53, *Hauptmann* Günther von Maltzahn, were successful. The afternoon escort sortie was different when, at 1555 hours, they took off to escort the bomb-laden Messerschmitt Bf 109s of

The final I/JG 53 recipient of the Kinght's Cross – Wolfgang Lippert, Staffel-kapitän of 3/JG 53 (second from the left) seen with left to right Uffz Karl Kühl, Oblt Julius Haase (killed in action 15 September 1940) and Fw Erich Kühlmann (killed in action 2 September 1940)

3/Erprobungsgruppe 210. The Staffel was to undertake many more of such *Jabo* or fighter bomber escort sorties before the Battle of Britain was over.

So far operations from the Pas de Calais had been successful with the objectives of the missions being met and seven (unconfirmed) air combat victories being achieved, not to mention the balloons shot down on the 31st of August. More importantly for the pilots no losses had been sustained but how much longer would this last. The odds were shortening and as the *1 Staffel* pilots woke up on the morning of Monday the 2nd of September 1940, some must have wondered if they would be seeing the same bed that evening.

At about 0700 hours *1 Staffel* drove from Le Touquet to Neuville to find the airfield shrouded in fog. The pilots began to relax but the German weather reconnaissance flights reported that contrary to what the pilots thought, the fog was only at ground level and ten metres above ground it was bright sunshine. Reassured about the weather, the Geschwader was then ordered to take off on a *Freie Jagd* fighter sweep between 4,000–5,000 metres altitude in support of bombing raids against targets in and around London and the Home Counties.

Tucked in behind his *Staffelkapitän* was *Unteroffizier* Werner Karl. Werner was surprised that the mission had not been scrubbed but taxied out behind Hans-Karl Mayer, whose fighter he could just about see in the gloom, opened his fighter's throttle and, at about 0717 hours, took to the air. The swirling dust cloud created by the eleven propellers of the *1 Staffel* fighters

Major *von Maltzahn*, Kommandeur, *II/JG 53 (centre), Le Touquet*

Left to right: Werner Karl, Willi Ghesla and Heinrich Höhnisch pose in front of Ghesla's 'White 12'

did not help conditions but no sooner had their undercarriages been retracted than the fighters flew out of the fog into a brilliant sunny sky.

The Staffel formed up into two *Schwarm* and a *Kette*, with Hans-Karl Mayer leading the first schwarm. However, mid way across the Channel and with the fighters still climbing, Hans-Karl Mayer reported that he was experiencing problems with his fighter's engine. Not wanting his engine to fail over enemy territory, he decided to return to Neuville and handed over command to *Oberleutnant* Hans Ohly. This was to have been Hans-Karl Mayer's last flight as *Staffelkapitän* as he was handing over the Staffel to Hans Ohly that afternoon so it must have been with a mixture of sadness and annoyance that Mayer-*Ast* hauled his fighter around and headed for home.

Hans Ohly was forced to re-arrange the Staffel formation and ordered Werner Karl, now without a *Rottenführer*, to the rear of the Staffel to form a *Deckungsrotte*. Reformed and settled, the Staffel continued on towards London without incident and on reaching the southern outskirts of the city, the German fighters wheeled around and, unchallenged, headed east towards Rochester. Soon after the RAF fighters attacked.

Werner Karl heard someone shout that enemy fighters were attacking from the west and not wanting to be bounced banked left in the hope of seeing the enemy. As he commenced the turn he glimpsed three RAF fighters screaming towards him. These fighters were possibly the three Hurricanes of 'Green Section, 253 Squadron. One of those pilots was

Flying Officer Alec Trueman who had shortly before tried to intercept the German bombers only to be attacked by the defending German fighters. Recovering from the initial German counter attack, he spotted a Messerschmitt Bf 109 over Rochester and managed to get behind it and fired two bursts lasting two to three seconds from 250 yards closing to 150 yards. After each burst, he saw bits fly off the German fighter's tail and fuselage but he was then forced to dive away when attacked by another Messerschmitt Bf 109. Alec Trueman did not see the fate of his opponent and could only claim the Messerschmitt as damaged.*

If it was Alec Trueman that had attacked Werner Karl, he had most certainly damaged the German aircraft. Unnoticed by the rest of *1 Staffel*, the first burst of fire hit the fuselage destroying the radio whilst the second burst again hit the fuselage and cockpit area, wounding Werner Karl on the back of his head. Shouting for help, he dived away not knowing that his Staffel were totally unaware of his fate. On recovering from the dive he could not see his assailants but could see the damage inflicted on his fighter so decided to head back to France. Setting a heading for Neuville, he settled down but remembering that there were still enemy aircraft about checked in his rear view mirror in case he was being followed. What he saw in the mirror was a Hurricane in an ideal firing position getting closer and closer.

Werner Karl slammed his control column over to the right and dived away, only levelling his wings when at about 200 metres above the Kent fields. Hoping that by hedgehopping he could throw off his pursuer's aim he did not know that this Hurricane was being flown by a pilot not much older than himself who had so far during the war shot down twelve and a half German aircraft and that this pilot intended making Werner Karl his next victory. Sergeant James 'Ginger' Lacey of 501 Squadron sat behind and slightly above Werner Karl shooting at the jinking German fighter with great skill. Taking his time, 'Ginger' Lacey's aim was good and Werner Karl, hearing the bullets hit his fighter, saw black and white smoke issue from the engine and the cockpit began to smell strongly of fuel. A line had been severed and fuel was pouring into the engine compartment and towards the cockpit. Scared that the next burst of fire would cause an explosion, Werner waited for the end. Looking again in the rear view mirror he could not see Lacey's Hurricane and scanning about him, he saw that it was flying to his right, just behind his crippled Messerschmitt. An attempt to climb in order to either bale out or ditch in the Channel resulted in his Messerschmitt's engine seizing and just short of the English Channel, Werner Karl's fighter eased itself gently on to the ground and, after hitting an anti-invasion pole, slithered to a stop a stone's throw from the Channel, just west of Hythe. All of this was witnessed by 'Ginger' Lacey who then headed north-east and landed at Gravesend just over ten minutes later, satisfied at having increased his score of

* Twenty-six-year-old Flying Officer Trueman was killed in action two days later – *Author*

victories to thirteen and a half.* Werner Karl remembers what followed clearly:

> I passed out soon after the crash-landing and when I regained consciousness, I found myself on a bed in a hut. Soldiers based on the coast had given me first aid. Later they told me that they were scared that I would have crashed into their hut. Soon, I could stand up and they allowed me to walk to the beach. At the water's edge I sat down and looked across the Channel towards France. I could see Luftwaffe aircraft returning to France, flying overhead and for the first time, I realised that I was a Prisoner of War; I had never felt so lonely and dejected in my life. Shortly after, a young Lieutenant came and sat by me. In very good German he told me that I would shortly be taken to a hospital. He tried to cheer me up and said 'You should be happy being in captivity and still living. You will survive the war but I am not so sure.' Soon after, I was collected by a captain and taken to a hospital within a barracks. After my wounds were treated, I was taken to Dover Castle. Then a short but considerate interrogation by an RAF officer followed and after staying the night in a cell, the next day I was taken to the Royal Herbert Hospital in Woolwich.

Werner Karl was to spend a short time in hospital but remembers receiving a big surprise soon after his arrival:

> As I walked towards my bed, I heard my name being shouted. I looked across to see a man with black skin. I did not know any black people and when he said his name was Josef and was from my Staffel, I thought it was a trick. Then I realised I was speaking to Josef Bröker and he was black because of his burns and the treatment he was receiving. This was the first I knew that he was alive.**

Werner Karl was not the only loss from *1 Staffel* on this day. That afternoon, the Staffel took off again on another escort sortie flying under the leadership of its new *Staffelkapitän* and *I Gruppe* under the leadership of its new *Gruppenkommandeur*. The flight was uneventful but although Luftwaffe records do not say so, it is believed that *Unteroffizier* Heinrich Rühl reported engine problems and was ordered to return to France by his *Staffelkapitän*. The radio conversation between Heinrich Rühl and Hans Ohly was heard by *Unteroffizier* Heinrich Höhnisch. What followed is described by Heinrich Höhnisch as being his most wonderful adventure as a fighter pilot – not an air combat victory but the saving of a friend:

> I was on my way back to France. In the distance, I could see a small dot with a black line behind it. When I got closer, I could see that it was one of our fighters with black smoke pouring from the engine. I could see it was Heinrich Rühl who was sitting in the cockpit having been told by the *Staffelkapitän* to throw off the roof. I flew besides him, waved my hand and waggled my wings. I flew higher to make sure that he was not attacked. The engine of his plane was still running but very slowly. It was more like a glider

---

* 'Ginger' Lacey was to survive the war. He was the RAF's eleventh highest scoring pilot of the war with at least twenty-eight victories – *Author*

** See Chapter Two – *Author*

and I showed him the way. The French Coast was visible through a brown-coloured haze but Heinrich was now too low. I could see the shadow of his plane on the water and he was flying closer and closer. Suddenly, there was a fountain of water and the Messerschmitt disappeared. Then the tail broke the surface and I could see that Heinrich had managed to get out of the cockpit. Immediately, the water was stained yellow and I flew around this spot to be sure that he was still alive and headed for France. My red fuel warning lamp had been glowing for about five minutes when I saw a motor-torpedo boat. In a case of such an emergency as this, we were ordered to fly over ships, waggle our wings and fly in the direction of the emergency. I flew to Rühl and back again, correcting the boat's course. I then saw a Dornier Do 18 with red cross markings. It would reach Rühl before the boat so I showed the pilot the direction and saw him land near Rühl just before I had to turn and landed with the last drops of fuel. Heinrich was picked up and taken to hospital where he had to stay for a few days because of hypothermia. When he came back, all the Staffel were pleased, especially me!

The 2nd of September 1940 was the worst day for *I Gruppe* so far during the Battle of Britain. In addition to the two losses suffered by *1 Staffel*, 3/JG 53 lost two pilots whilst a third *3 Staffel* pilot crash-landed his fighter at Boulogne. The Gruppe did claim four victories with *Hauptmann* Hans-Karl Mayer claiming his first as *Gruppenkommandeur* and *Hauptmann* Lippert his last as *Staffelkapitän* of 3/JG 53. *Oberfeldwebel* Erich Kühlmann scored his fourth victory only to be one of the two *3 Staffel* losses shortly afterwards.

Uffz Rühl (centre) flanked on his left by Lt Zeis and on his right Lt Schultz

The final victory for the Gruppe went to *Leutnant* Ernst-Albrecht Schultz of *1 Staffel* but this cannot be confirmed. Celebrations for these victories must have been muted as the new *Staffelkapitän* of 1 and 3/JG 53 had the task of preparing letters to the next of kin of those missing and the new *Gruppenkommandeur* had to report to his *Geschwaderkommodore* the loss of four aircraft and three pilots with a further aircraft damaged and two pilots in hospital.

The week that followed was a very busy if not uneventful one for *1 Staffel*, flying at least twice a day on such tasks as escorting air sea rescue float planes, Messerschmitt Bf 109 *Jabos* and the increasing number of bomber escorts. The Staffel scored eight victories during this period but no documentary evidence exists as to what types were claimed and at what times. The only mission of note occurred on the 8th of September and seemed to be witnessed by most of the Luftwaffe flying that day, not only *1 Staffel*. *Oberleutnant* Heinz-Eugen Wittmeyer had recently become *Gruppenadjutant* of I/JG 53, replacing *Oberleutnant* Julius Haase who had taken command of 3/JG 53. The Gruppe had taken off just before lunch on an escort mission for Heinkel He 111s. The *Gruppenschwarm* leading the formation with the other three *Staffeln* at varying heights behind. The RAF put up little opposition to this formation and when Heinz Wittmeyer spotted three aircraft they turned out to be from 8/JG 53, not the RAF. Having turned towards them, Hans-Karl Mayer confirmed that they were friendly and allowed them to approach. It was normal in such encounters

Happy times – Heinz Wittmeyer (far right) with fellow pilots from 2/JG 53 (left to right Lt Günther Hess, Oblt Rudi Schmidt and Fw Hans Kornatz)

for the smaller formation to give way to the larger which is what two of the three *8 Staffel* aircraft did. However, the *Staffelkapitän, Oberleutnant* Heinz Kunert, an experienced pilot with nine victories, did not give way and what happened next was witnessed by many of the German aircrew flying that day. Heinz Wittmeyer remembers it clearly:

> I tried in the last second to avoid disaster and pushed my stick forward but it was too late, especially for the other pilot. Both fighters disintegrated and I found myself falling through the sky without my plane. I opened my parachute but found myself virtually blind (later in a field hospital they removed twenty metal splinters from my right eye and six from my left). There was a strong north-westerly wind that day which blew me towards the French Coast. When I hit the water, I tried to release myself from the parachute but could not which was good because the parachute acted like a kite and I became one of the first windsurfers. The kite brought me nearer the coast but on becoming wetter and wetter, the parachute eventually collapsed. I then managed to get free and swam towards France for nearly an hour after which I was helped by soldiers who came out to me. The other pilot was not so lucky. It appeared that when we collided, one propeller blade of the other Messerschmitt cut my cockpit in front of my head, the next blade hit behind my head cutting the seat belts and my shoulder.

Although he did not think so at the time, Heinz Wittmeyer was a very lucky man. He returned to JG 53 in the middle of 1941 but found that his right eye had been too badly damaged for him to continue flying as a fighter pilot. Accordingly, he served on a number of ground appointments for the remainder of the war . . . no trace was ever found of Heinz Kunert.

1 Staffel did not have to wait long for its next mission. On the following day the Staffel was briefed for yet another escort mission. By now the Staffel was beginning to dislike such missions, as recalled by *Unteroffizier* Willi Ghesla:

> We much preferred the *Freie Jagd*. Close escort was unpleasant and we were always in an unfavourable position when attacked by the RAF.

A similar view was expressed by *Feldwebel* Heinrich Höhnisch. In January 1940, he had joined *1 Staffel* and so far had enjoyed a successful War, achieving six victories and having only once been damaged in combat. Added to that score a number of balloons shot down on the 30th and 31st of August 1940, Heinrich Höhnisch was regarded as one of the 'old hands' of the Staffel. He was not to know what lay ahead for him as the Geschwader took off on its only mission, at about 1655 hours on Monday the 9th of September as part of the escort for a bombing raid against targets in and around London Docks.

One of the German bomber pilots being escorted by JG 53 was *Oberfeldwebel* Oskar Broderix of *Stab* III/KG 53. For him this was his fiftieth operational flight and he was so confident that he had brought along his camera to photograph the other Heinkel He 111s in his formation and the results of their bombs. Having picked up their escort, he and his

*Heinrich Höhnisch (left)
with his mechanic*

Geschwader headed for their target – the Queen Elizabeth Docks,
confident of another successful mission.*

After crossing the Kent Coast it was not long before the bombers were
engaged by a tenacious defence mounted by Spitfires and Hurricanes.
However, at the back of the formation *1 Staffel* was not immediately
engaged in combat. Three of the Heinkels they were meant to escort had
become separated from the main bomber formation and *Oberleutnant* Hans
Ohly was forced to break his Staffel away from the rest of JG 53 to look

---

* Oskar Broderix succeeded in reaching the target on what would be his last operational
flight. Soon after dropping his bombs, he was attacked by Hurricanes of 605 Squadron.
Having shot down one Hurricane, another, flown by Pilot Officer George Forrester,
collided with his Heinkel, severing the tail of the German bomber. Only Broderix and his
observer survived – *Author*

after them. Approaching the target, Heinrich Höhnisch, flying in the unenviable position of one of the *Deckungsrotte* with another experienced former Condor Legion pilot, *Oberfeldwebel* Alfred Müller, was getting very concerned that they would soon be turning back the way they had come and would be looking directly into the sun, an ideal situation for being bounced. The bombers dropped their load, the formation wheeled about and on setting a course for France, exactly what Heinrich Höhnisch hoped would not happen did.

Looking ahead Heinrich saw with alarm six Spitfires on a converging course, coming out of the sun. Opening his fighter's throttle, he tried to draw level and above the Schwarm headed by *Oberleutnant* Hans Ohly with the intention of breaking up the Spitfires' attack. He thought that he had succeeded but all of a sudden he heard a rattling sound as bullets hit his Messerschmitt; his fighter then exploded in a mass of flames and Heinrich Höhnisch felt as if his face was being scorched by a blow-lamp. Yet again, the *Deckungsrotte* had saved the Staffel at the expense of one of its number. Acting as top cover to his Staffel without top cover himself, Heinrich had been bounced from behind by an unseen and even today unknown RAF pilot.

Heinrich Höhnisch now struggled to get free from the inferno and eventually succeeded in throwing off the canopy roof, releasing his seat straps and falling out of the blazing aircraft. On opening his parachute, only then did he realise that he had severe burns to his face and hands and that he had been hit by a bullet in his right leg. Having baled out at about 22,000

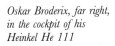

Oskar Broderix, far right, in the cockpit of his Heinkel He 111

feet, he took some time to come down by parachute, eventually landing near Tatsfield in Kent. Bring in no fit state to take evasive action he was captured. Despite his severe burns, he was interrogated soon after admission to hospital but impressed his interrogators by 'giving away absolutely no information regarding his unit'. However, his fighter gave away more information as, having crashed on the edge of the airfield at Biggin Hill, RAF experts were able to take their time in sifting through the wreckage in the hope of finding clues to its unit or information that might help the RAF fighter plots. Not much was left of Heinrich's 'White 5' but on the underside of one of the wings, towards the trailing edge, they found two small discs about the size of a penny, painted like an RAF roundel and inscribed '13.8.40' and looking to be patches covering bullet holes. Their assumption was correct and Heinrich can today reveal the reasons for such unusual markings:

> On the 13th of August 1940, I was hit by machine gun fire in my starboard wing by a Hurricane which came up behind me. I was forced by him to roll and dive away but he chased me at sea level all the way back to Cherbourg when he turned away.

Meanwhile, back at 22,000 feet, the Staffel had become embroiled in a series of dogfights. One of the German pilots, *Feldwebel* Herbert Tzschoppe, had become separated from his *Rottenführer*, *Leutnant* Ernst-Albrecht Schultz, whom he last saw shooting down a Hurricane on the eastern outskirts of London before both of them were attacked themselves. Deciding to head back to France and safety, he noticed below him two Hurricanes apparently oblivious of the danger that still existed in the skies. Making sure that there was nothing behind him he attacked the right hand Hurricane with such effect that the RAF fighter disintegrated, its pilot baling out. The other Hurricane dived away and at that same instant, to his alarm, Herbert Tzschoppe realised that there was another aircraft coming alongside him. Alarm was soon replaced by relief when he recognised the code 'White 2' on what turned out to be the Messerschmitt Bf 109 of *Leutnant* Schultz. Schultz had witnessed the combat ensuring that Herbert Tzschoppe's third victory of the war was confirmed. In addition to Schultz and Tzschoppe's victories one was also claimed by another *1 Staffel* pilot, *Unteroffizier* Heinrich Kopperschläger (though unconfirmed), another by Hans-Karl Mayer and a further four victories claimed by pilots from *9 Staffel*. Each of the three *Gruppen* of JG 53 suffered one fighter lost and the only survivor, albeit badly wounded, was Heinrich Höhnisch.

The days that followed were quiet for both the Luftwaffe and *1 Staffel*. Bad weather on the 10th of September resulted in some of the Staffel flying as an escort for a convoy of ships without incident, whilst the long awaited *Freie Jagd* flown over the English Coast on Wednesday the 11th of September finished both without victory or loss.

The RAF's attempts to combat the build-up of the German invasion fleet resulted in the Staffel's next action on the afternoon of the 12th of September. At 1545 hours three Bristol Blenheim Mark VIs of 59

Squadron had taken off from the airfield at Thorney Island escorted by three Blenheim Mark VIA fighters of 235 Squadron. Off Le Havre they spotted fifteen motor vessels and attacked. This convoy consisted of fourteen steamers escorted by the warship *August Bolten* all of which narrowly avoided being sunk when all the bombs missed. A heavy anti-aircraft battery at Le Havre opened fire and forced three of the Blenheims to head back towards the safety of England. However, the 59 Squadron and 235 Squadron Blenheims, the latter Squadron's aircraft being flown by Flying Officer Douglas Wordsworth, Sergeant Harold Sutton and Flight Sergeant Dick Nelson, had been spotted by a lone Messerschmitt Bf 109 whose pilot, *Leutnant* Alfred Zeis, relates the following:

> I had been on a ferrying flight from Rennes to Le Touquet and was flying along the coast. The weather was bad with almost total low-lying cloud cover. Just before I reached Le Havre, I saw some fountains on the edge of the harbour basin and saw three planes heading for the clouds, one after the other. At full throttle I tried to intercept before they could reach the cloud and just before the last one disappeared, I expended all my 20mm ammunition against him without success, the range was too great. I followed the last plane into cloud flying on instruments, and came up behind three Blenheims flying close together. I first shot at the engines of the left-hand Blenheim and then attacked the right hand one before they disappeared into cloud but not before my Messerschmitt had received several hits. Before they

Lt Schultz *(right) and Lt* Zeis *relax between missions*

had disappeared I saw the effect of some of my fire which was black smoke coming from one of the planes.

By now, I decided to turn back and on instruments flew towards Le Havre between two layers of clouds. Suddenly, a second flight of three Blenheims appeared in front of me flying on a reciprocal course to me. I dived and shot at them whilst they climbed and shot at me. I was hit again and now tried to land at Le Havre-Octeville airfield. The visibility at the airfield was not good and was not helped by my windscreen being covered in oil. I did manage to land and had to leave the Messerschmitt there as the engine had to be changed and the holes repaired. In my combat report, I said that at least one Blenheim had been damaged but when I was asked, I did not completely exclude a kill but as none of those Blenheims had been hit by 20mm ammunition, I felt that a kill was questionable.

Two witnesses, the Captains of the *August Bolten* and another warship, *H47*, said that they had seen the combats but could not say whether any of the Blenheims had crashed. Nonetheless Alfred Zeis was credited with his tenth victory. All six Blenheims returned, the rear gunners of the 235 Squadron Blenheims convinced that they had driven off the Messerschmitt and had damaged it. Surprisingly, Luftwaffe records, normally very meticulous, do not make any mention of this combat or the damage to the Messerschmitt.

The 14th of September saw both *I* and *II Gruppe* taking a day of rest,

In its blast pen at Etaples, the rudder of Alfred Zeis's 'White 3' shows ten victories (his tenth being a Blenheim on 12 September 1940)

I Gruppe preparing themselves for the move from Neuville to the airfield at Etaples scheduled for the following day. Sunday the 15th of September was destined to see the Luftwaffe launching its heaviest attack of the whole Battle of Britain and from this day on would be celebrated in Britain as 'Battle of Britain Day', the Germans, who were to suffer a crushing defeat, must have cursed the day. Most Luftwaffe units were to be heavily committed throughout the day and JG 53 was no exception.

Having completed the move to Etaples earlier in the morning, the Staffel took off at 1103 hours on an escort mission for the Dornier Do 17s of I and III/KG 76 who were attacking targets in London. The omens for *1 Staffel* were not good as seventeen minutes after taking off the *Staffelkapitän*, *Oberleutnant* Hans Ohly landed back at Etaples because his radio had failed. Leadership of the Staffel was handed over to the most experienced pilot who happened to be a non-commissioned officer, *Oberfeldwebel* Alfred 'Mollinero' Müller, and the Staffel continued unchecked towards London.

The *Deckungsrotte* on this mission was *Feldwebel* Herbert Tzschoppe and *Unteroffizier* Heinrich Kopperschläger. Due to aircraft unserviceability, Herbert Tzschoppe was not flying his usual Messerschmitt Bf 109 coded 'White 4' and inscribed with the name of his fiancée Annelies, whom he was due to marry at the end of the month, but the new plane of the injured *Gruppenadjutant* Heinz Wittmeyer. In an unfamiliar plane flying in the *Deckungsrotte*, the Staffel, flying at the back of the escorting formation and the *Staffelkapitän* back on the ground at Etaples, the omens were definitely

Ofw *Alfred Müller (second from right) with (left to right) Heinrich Kopperschläger, Werner Karl and Willi Ghesla*

getting worse. To worry him further, the bombers were flying exceptionally slowly and to keep in formation, Herbert remembers that they had to fly with their flaps down, making them easy pickings for the defending RAF fighters.

Without warning the German formation was attacked out of the sun and, in one of the first bursts, the *1 Staffel* pilots saw the aircraft of the temporary *Staffelkapitän* hit and dive away. Alfred Müller was heard to say that he had been hit in the arm then nothing more was heard. It is thought that Müller managed to make it to the Channel but crashed into the sea; he was captured but no records exist as to where. Meanwhile, Herbert Tzschoppe had been attacked by a Spitfire, presumably from 41 Squadron who were based at Hornchurch in Essex, and had been hit in the wings. Separated from his *Rottenflieger* and the rest of the German formation he decided that he would head back to France as he was not sure how badly damaged his fighter was. Today he admits that another reason for returning was wanting to ensure that he was alive to marry Annelies who was also carrying their child. Using the clouds he flew from one to another but unfortunately for him, not knowing that he had been seen, he was being stalked by a Spitfire.

Flying Officer Tony Lovell of 41 Squadron was a dedicated fighter pilot and remembered by many who flew with him as a 'loner'. He had four and a half victories so far during the war and had the dubious honour of being wounded by *Major* Werner Mölders, former *Staffelkapitän* of 1/JG 53 and now *Kommodore* of JG 51, on the 28th of July 1940. He had also been shot down on the 5th of September 1940 but, unwounded, returned to flying

41 Squadron during the early part of the Battle of Britain; Tony Lovell is second row third from the right

the following day, claiming retribution by shooting down a Messerschmitt Bf 110.

Flying Officer Lovell had spotted the lone Messerschmitt turn east and dive away and had stalked the unwary German for fifteen miles before opening fire and hitting it in the port wing. In the Messerschmitt, Herbert Tzschoppe threw off the canopy roof and, without thinking, undid his seat belts as if expecting the worse. Herbert now thinks that this saved his life as Tony Lovell fired two more bursts and saw the German fighter catch fire. Herbert saw flames burst from the instrument panel like an oxyacetylene torch and they quickly caused severe burns to his hands and face. Immediately after, his fighter exploded and threw him out of the cockpit – the next thing that Herbert remembers was that he was hanging on his parachute.

Herbert Tzschoppe was lucky to be alive and the fact that he had thrown off the canopy roof and undone his seat straps had saved his life. Below him, he could see the burning remains of his fighter hit the ground three miles south-east of Canterbury and, as he looked up, saw that he was being circled by two Spitfires, the pilot of one saluted him to which Herbert

Herbert Tzschoppe (photo taken after his capture)

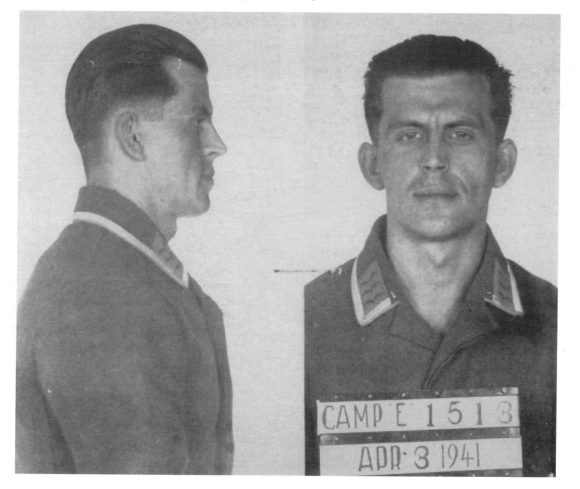

returned the compliment. Meanwhile on the ground, eighteen year old John Sampson, out shooting in his local woods with a friend, heard the sound of a dogfight and looked up to see Herbert hanging on his parachute. The German soon landed in a tree and on releasing himself fell to the ground hurting his knees. Looking up he could see John Sampson and his friend, both armed with shotguns, standing close by and he immediately surrendered to them, handing over his flare pistol with great difficulty because of his burned hands, just as locally billeted New Zealand soldiers arrived. Seeing that his job was done, Tony Lovell flew over the group and headed back towards Hornchurch.

Herbert was soon taken to hospital where his burns were treated with both skill and compassion. Three days later he was visited by an army major who promised to send a letter to Annelies. The letter arrived exactly three months after he was shot down and was positive proof to Annelies that her fiancé was alive and that the wedding could be rearranged, when the war permitted! Annelies and Herbert were married by proxy in 1941 and he had to wait a further six years before he could kiss his new bride and daughter!

Back in the skies above Kent, the pilots of *I Gruppe* were fighting for their lives. In addition to the two fighters lost by *1 Staffel*, another aircraft had been damaged and was limping back to crash land at Etaples. *2 Staffel* had lost two pilots; *Unteroffizier* Hans Schersand failed to return while the popular *Oberleutnant* Rudolf 'Kleine' Schmidt succeeded in baling out but

Uffz. Hans Schersand, killed in action 15 September 1940

Oblt *(seen here as* Lt)
Rudolf Schmidt, killed in
action 15 September
1940

was killed when his parachute failed to open. *3 Staffel* lost its new
Staffelkapitän, Oberleutnant Julius Haase (again he baled out but was killed
when his parachute failed to open) and *Unteroffizier* Karl-Heinz Feldmann
crash-landed near the coast and was taken prisoner.

JG 53 were to claim a total of fourteen RAF fighters in this action. *1 Staffel*
made up for the loss of two of their pilots by claiming four RAF fighters.
Unteroffizier Willi Ghesla had spotted what he thought was a Spitfire
attacking a Messerschmitt Bf 109 and closing unseen to within eighty

metres opened fire setting fire to the fighter whose pilot baled out. His likely victim was Flying Officer Arthur Nesbitt of 1 Squadron, Royal Canadian Air Force (RCAF) whose Hurricane was shot down near Tunbridge Wells, Nesbitt baling out wounded. Another Hurricane of 1 Squadron, RCAF probably fell to the guns of another *1 Staffel* pilot, *Unteroffizier* Heinrich Kopperschläger, but this time, its pilot Flying Officer Ross Smither was killed when his fighter crashed at Staplehurst. The remaining *1 Staffel* victories were claimed by Willi Ghesla and *Leutnant* Ernst-Albrecht Schultz but cannot be substantiated.

The day did not end there for *1 Staffel* and neither did the victories. With *Oberleutnant* Hans Ohly back in command, the Staffel took off again with the rest of the Geschwader at 1345 hours on yet another escort sortie, this time for the Dornier Do 17s of II and II/KG 2 in their attack on the Surrey Commercial Dock in London and targets 'of opportunity' in and around London. Shortly before reaching the target two squadrons of RAF fighters were seen to attack the bombers and when they became too engrossed, 1/JG 53 was able to bounce the rearmost RAF fighters. Although the attack was headed by the *Staffelkapitän*, it was his *Rottenflieger, Unteroffizier* Heinrich Rühl who claimed one 'Spitfire' and *Unteroffizier* Heinrich Kopperschläger who claimed another, both kills being logged at 1450 hours. Their victims were probably the Hurricanes of 303 Squadron who lost two aircraft at about the same time; Sergeant Michal Brzezowski was presumed to have been killed when he was shot down into the Thames Estuary whilst Sergeant Tadeusz Andruszkow was luckier in that he managed to bale out of his crippled fighter over the Isle of Grain.

The Staffel returned much happier seventy-five minutes after taking off and this time all the aircraft returned safely. It had been a far more successful mission with the rest of *I Gruppe* claiming a further four victories, *II Gruppe* claiming two unconfirmed kills and *II Gruppe* claiming another four victories. *III Gruppe* lost two fighters, one running out of fuel and the other crashing on landing on its return to Etaples. In both cases the pilot survived.*

If *1 Staffel* thought the day was over, they were wrong for at 1755 hours, they were scrambled to intercept an incoming raid which was believed to be the Blenheims of 53 Squadron which were attacking shipping off Boulogne; twenty minutes later, the Staffel landed without contact with the RAF.

For both sides the remainder of the Battle of Britain would be nothing compared to this day. In fact although *1 Staffel* was to fly virtually every single day up to the end of September 1940 no claims were made or aircraft lost. The whole Geschwader claimed thirty-two victories in between the 16th and 30th of September 1940 and of those victories only five were claimed by *I Gruppe*. *Oberleutnant* Hans Ohly's log book records a total of seventeen operational flights ranging from escorting bombers and fighter

---

* It cannot be ascertained for certain whether the III/JG 53 losses occurred during the first or second mission of the day – *Author*

bombers, *Freie Jagd* missions, convoy escort and one scramble. The opportunity was there but luck was not with them.

Still in the front line, those pilots must have now reflected on the losses of their friends during the month. Four pilots had been shot down and were missing and it was not until November 1940 that the Red Cross informed the Geschwader that all four were prisoners-of-war. The pilot's fears must have been reinforced when the body of *Feldwebel* Heinrich Bezner was washed ashore at Boulogne nearly a month after going missing off Portsmouth. For *Unteroffizier* Willi Ghesla, he was the only one left out of his band of friends and now had quite a collection of pistols. However, he recalls that the pilots did not try to dwell on such morbid thought:

> Some of the ground crew tried to blame the pilots for their attitude: 'We cannot understand how you can still laugh while your comrades are dead or missing' they would say. If we had thought about it, it would have been impossible to keep on flying.

For other pilots, the thought of another mission brought on a bout of *Kanalkrankheit*, literally, 'Channel sickness'. At the end of the mission brief, nearly all pilots would head to the latrines and, in some cases, briefings had even taken place around the toilet. Nobody talked about it, it was expected.

However, for *1 Staffel*, the Battle of Britain was by no means over. Losses would continue, one of which would come as a great shock to the Staffel, and they were destined not to increase its score of ninety-one aircraft shot down. Heinrich Kopperschläger's kill on the 15th of September was to be the last for 1940 and in fact the Staffel was not to claim a single enemy aircraft for the next nine months. The Luftwaffe's final phase of the Battle was about to start and *1 Staffel* still had a part to play.

CHAPTER TEN

A Most Remarkable Man – Exemplary in Every Respect

Towards the end of September 1940 the number of *Jabo* sorties began to increase dramatically. In addition to the Messerschmitt Bf 110s and Bf 109s of *Erprobungsgruppe 210* and Messerschmitt Bf 109s of *Lehrgeschwader 2* (LG 2), both units having been involved in fighter bomber sorties since the start of the Battle of Britain, all the *Jagdgeschwadern* now had to designate certain Staffeln as *Jabostaffeln*. JG 53 was no exception with *3, 4* and *8 Staffeln* (one from each of the Gruppe) being designated as the Geschwader's fighter-bomber Staffeln.

Jabo training for *I Gruppe* had begun shortly after the 15th of September. *3 Staffel* was now commanded by *Oberleutnant* Walter Rupp, a former *1 Staffel* pilot who had been badly injured on the 10th of May 1940 when his fighter had been rammed by another *1 Staffel* aircraft which was flown by *Unteroffizier* Ludwig Reibel. Both he and Reibel (who was shot down and taken prisoner by the French on the 25th of May) had recently returned to *I Gruppe* but Walter Rupp now took command of *3 Staffel* following the death of *Oberleutnant* Julius Haase on the 15th of September. The Messerschmitt Bf 109 *Jabos* were armed with a single 250kg bomb and to practice, cement bombs were used against targets off the beach at Le Touquet with varying degrees of success. *Feldwebel* Hans Kornatz of *2 Staffel* (presumably the other Staffeln were given the chance of practising *Jabo* techniques) returned to Etaples after one practice flight to be told that he had missed the target by 250 metres and had hit the Le Touquet Cemetery! However, the views of the JG 53 pilots on having their fighters weighed down by a bomb is best summed up by *Gefreiter* Heinz Zag who had arrived on 8/JG 53 in the first week of September, expecting to be a fighter pilot:

> I flew one of the first Bf 109s in the Staffel which was modified to carry a 250kg bomb. However, the Staffel was not properly trained which concerned me. I did not think it was a good idea – we had a short enough flying range before being weighed down by a bomb!

The first *Jabo* mission for JG 53 took place on Wednesday the 2nd of October. *1 Staffel* was to fly three escort missions for, as *Oberleutnant* Hans Ohly described, 'Bf 109 bombers'. In glorious blue skies and flying at a high altitude, the first raid crossed the Kent Coast shortly after 0930 hours and headed for London. It was an uneventful mission for *1 Staffel*, who saw

3/JG 53 – the Jabostaffel. *Standing, left to right:* Uffz *Alexander Bleymüller,* Fhr *Walter Seiz,* Lt *Wolfgang Tonne,* Oblt *Walter Rupp (*Staffelkapitän*). Front:* Lt *Karl Leonhard and* Uffz *Alfred Baumer. The bomb is inscribed 'The 3rd Staffel Greets London'*

nothing, but III/JG 53 had the misfortune of meeting the RAF and losing its *Gruppenadjutant*, the *Staffelkapitän* and two other pilots of 8/JG 53 – *8 Staffel* being the Jabostaffel of *III Gruppe*. One of the pilots lost was *Gefreiter* Heinz Zag who was only flying on his seventh mission. Flying in his Staffel leader's *Kette*, they were bounced by Spitfires of 603 Squadron who shot down all three *Jabos*. Heinz Zag's fighter was hit in the engine and when it seized-up, he tried to glide back to France. Out of luck, he was forced to crash-land near the Kent village of Goudhurst, his virtually intact fighter giving the RAF Intelligence the opportunity to investigate a relatively new fighter bomber, having soon discovered it was fitted with a bomb rack.

The afternoon sorties were more successful with *1 Staffel* this time escorting the *Jabos* of II/LG 2 without incident, resulting in *II Fliegerkorps*

declaring that *Jabo* operations were a success. This was to set the scene for the remainder of the Battle of Britain.

3/JG 53 'Emil' with its bomb, Le Touquet, October 1940

The following two days were quiet, allowing the *Staffelkapitän* to check out one of the Staffel's new pilots, *Fähnrich* Walter Zellot. The next mission was scheduled for the morning of the 5th of October when they would be escorting the Messerschmitt Bf 110s of *1* and *2/Erprobungsgruppe 210* in their attacks against Becton Gasworks and the airfield at West Malling. One pilot, *Unteroffizier* Willi Ghesla, was excused the mission as during the previous twenty-four hours he had been on guard duty. As dawn broke, the poor weather looked as if it would hamper the mission but at 1055 hours, the Staffel were airborne, meeting up with the Messerschmitt Bf

250kg bomb on a 3/JG 53 'Emil'

110s just after they had taken off from their forward airfield at Calais-Marck.

Willi Ghesla was not relaxing back in his barracks. As the Staffel was short of pilots, due to sickness, and they would not be penetrating inland from Dover it was decided that it was safe for him to fly. The ground crew, thinking that Ghesla would not be flying, were servicing his 'White 12' which meant he was given *Unteroffizier* Heinrich Rühl's 'White 10' to fly as Rühl was sick and not flying.

On reaching Dover the Staffel was ordered to continue towards London, presumably to escort *1/Erprobungsgruppe 210* closer to their target. Shortly after the formation of Messerschmitt Bf 109s and 110s was intercepted by

the Hurricanes of 303, 501 and 1 (RCAF) Squadrons. 303 and 501 Squadron attacked the fighter bombers while 1 Squadron, RCAF took on the Messerschmitt Bf 109s. One of the Canadian pilots was Flying Officer Paul Pitcher who recalls the first of three patrols he was to fly that day:

Unusual markings on the bomb rack of a 3/JG 53 'jabo'

> My log book reveals the following entry in relation to the sortie: 'Hurricane coded YO-D, patrol Northolt and Dover. Me 109s and 110s engaged; one Me 109 destroyed, engaged and damaged one Me 110. Port fuel tank hit.'
> It was an extremely busy hour and five minutes and positive recollection of details is difficult. However, as far as I recall the 109's undercarriage dropped down and I reported this to the Intelligence Officer on landing.

Willi Ghesla in the cockpit of his fighter

However, my most vivid impression of that sortie was the landing at Northolt. My aircraft did not have self-sealing fuel tanks and my port fuel tank was riddled with bullet holes and the cockpit awash with fuel. The air turbulence of landing caused clouds of fuel to swirl over the engine cowling and hot exhaust stacks but, by some miracle, the aircraft failed to explode.

Leutnant Alfred Zeis of 1/JG 53 had been separated from his *Rottenflieger* following the bounce by the RAF fighters and desperately tried to identify friend and foe in the mass of wheeling aircraft. He spotted a Messerschmitt from *1 Staffel* being attacked by a Hurricane and dived to protect his comrade. As the Hurricane broke away, he himself was attacked from behind and his fighter took many hits in the engine, radiator and flying controls. Added to this his undercarriage dropped down and he found it increasingly difficult to control his fighter. With no *Rottenflieger* and an unresponsive aircraft, he tried in vain to get away from his attacker, possibly the Canadian Paul Pitcher*, who continued to fire as the opportunity arose. During a desperate turn to get away, the engine stopped and the Messerschmitt went into a spin. Zeis, try as he might, could not regain control so he threw off the canopy roof and baled out his 'White 3', a veteran of so many combats and sporting ten victory bars on the rudder, disintegrated on hitting the ground four miles west of Ashford.

* Sergeant Siudak of 303 Squadron also claimed a Messerschitt Bf 109 destroyed near Ashford – *Author*

The pilot of the German fighter that Alfred Zeis tried to help was also in trouble. Willi Ghesla recalls what happened to him:

I was flying in the *Deckungsrotte* at about 8,000 metres altitude just below some clouds. Suddenly RAF fighters appeared out of the clouds and before I could dive away, I was hit in the engine and oil-cooler. I dived to 4,000 metres, regained control and set course for Calais as my engine was seizing. I was then attacked a second time and lost consciousness for a short time. When I came to, I found myself close to the ground and so looked for somewhere to land. With few alternatives, I found a small meadow and landed. During the landing, I hit my head on the gunsight because I had released my seat harness instead of my parachute and again, I lost consciousness. When I regained consciousness a second time, the aircraft had stopped and all was quiet. I climbed out and walked to a nearby farmhouse where, shortly afterwards, I was captured.

For the second time in the Battle of Britain the RAF had a perfect example of a *1 Staffel* aircraft and this time they submitted Willi's aircraft to very close scrutiny as the following report reveals:

Messerschmitt 109E-4, crashed 5 Oct 50, at New Bank Farm, Bilsington. Markings '10' in white. Nose and rudder yellow. Aircraft built by Bayerische Flugzeugwerke number 1804. Acceptance date 3 Aug 38. Daimler Benz 601 built by DB Genshagen Teltow. Armament 2x MG 17 and 2x 20mm

Lt *Alfred Zeis standing by 'White 4', the aircraft normally flown by* Fw *Tzschoppe*

cannon. Armour: cross bulkhead in fuselage but cockpit roof had been jettisoned. Following fighter action, aircraft force landed. There are a number of 303 strikes in tail, fuselage, wing and engine appears to have overheated indicating damage to cooler system. Pilot prisoner-of-war, slightly wounded. Camouflage grey, dappled black, carefully done.

Willi's fighter was taken away and later used in displays and raised money and morale in and around London in the following weeks and months.

Who shot down Willi Ghesla is not known as, excluding Paul Pitcher's claim, 1 Squadron, RCAF claimed a further two Messerschmitt Bf 109s destroyed (Flying Officer Beverley Christmas and Flight Lieutenant Gordon McGregor) and two more damaged while 303 Squadron claimed four destroyed (Sergeant Stanislaw Karubin, Sergeant Jan Palak claiming one each, Sergeant Antoni Siudak claiming two) and two damaged. Even 501 Squadron filed claims with one destroyed by Pilot Officer Kenneth Mackenzie and another damaged. JG 53 lost the two fighters from *1 Staffel* while the *Staffelkapitän* of 7/JG 53, *Oberleutnant* Heinz Altendorf, managed to return to France with a badly damaged aircraft which was written off in a crash-landing. A further two fighters from other units crashed in the Channel, their pilots being rescued. One pilot who could have possibly damaged Willi Ghesla's fighter in the first attack was Flying Officer Hartland Molson of 1 Squadron, RCAF who, for reasons that will become obvious, was to remember the 5th of October very well:

I found a pair of Messerschmitt 109s working together. I chased them around for a few minutes getting in short bursts whenever the sights were on. One was damaged and went down. I started on the second and it seemed to slow up and straighten out. At this point I forgot all I had learned because I slowed up and straightened out too – without looking around. There was a gentleman behind just hoping that I would do something stupid and he knocked my machine out of control with his little cannon in about two seconds. A moment later I was off on the greatest fight of my life, strictly on my own; trying to bale out at 23,000 feet. By the time I had got out the plane had dropped some 2,000 feet and was travelling at about 400 miles an hour which made our parting doubly uncomfortable. However, the rotten sensation left when I had slowed down to a terminal velocity of about 125 miles per hour. I dropped 11,000 feet before pulling the rip-cord and landed in some woods where a fir tree broke my fall. This spoiled my efforts to follow the proper instructions for landing and the first part of me which made contact with the ground was my bottom.

A detachment of the First Kensingtons came through a ride in the woods and took me to the casualty clearing station at Chartham where the medical officer dressed my wounds. The following day the medical officer came down from Northolt with an ambulance and took me to the Canadian Hospital at Taplow.

303 Squadron lost one Hurricane, its pilot being killed, whilst 603 Squadron lost a Spitfire in the same area at the same time. Claims were filed by *Oberleutnant* Walter Rupp from *3 Staffel* (though this was uncon-firmed), two pilots from *II Gruppe* and one from *III Gruppe*. It is only

conjecture that Hartland Molson damaged Willi Ghesla and was possibly shot down by Alfred Zeis as there was no time or opportunity to witness the fate of the Hurricane attacking the fighter.

Although *1 Staffel* escorted *3 Staffel* on a *Jabo* mission later that afternoon, it was not able to avenge the loss of two of its more experienced pilots. The Staffel had now lost nearly a third of its aircraft in action so far in the Battle of Britain but, unusually, only one pilot had died. The days that now followed would be monotonous, mainly escorting *3 Staffel* over the next twelve days without loss or luck. When the next loss came, it was to be for the Geschwader, and especially the pilots of *1 Staffel*, their greatest shock and saddest loss of the war so far.

The Geschwader was heavily committed on Thursday the 17th of October with the Staffeln of each of the three Gruppen escorting their respective *Jabostaffeln*. *1 Staffel* took off at 0840 hours escorting *Oberleutnant* Walter Rupp's fighter bombers and their bombs were dropped between Margate and London. Although one pilot from 7/JG 53 claimed to have shot down a Spitfire, the majority of the Geschwader returned without incident.

Later that afternoon the whole Geschwader took off again on a similar *Jabo* mission and again, the target was London. This time, both *I* and *II Gruppe* were involved in combat. *III Gruppe* was attacked on the return flight near Tonbridge by, according to them, twelve Spitfires who badly damaged the fighters of *Oberleutnant* Robert Magath of 7/JG 53 and *Oberleutnant* Ernst-Günther Heinze, the new *Staffelkapitän* of 8/JG 53. Magath managed to fly his crippled aircraft back to France whilst Heinze ditched in the Channel and was soon rescued. Only *Feldwebel* Eduard Koslowski of *8 Staffel* claimed to have shot down one of the attacking Spitfires.

A similar sequence of events happened to *I Gruppe*. The Gruppe had taken off at about 1440 hours – *Oberleutnant* Walter Rupp's fighter bombers were again to attack an unspecified target in London and would be protected by the fighters of *Oberleutnant* Hans Ohly's *1 Staffel* and *Oberleutnant* Ignatz Prestelle's *2 Staffel*. For some unknown reason, *Hautmann* Hans-Karl Mayer was not leading his Gruppe on this mission, leadership of the Gruppe being given to Ignatz Prestelle. Mayer had recently returned from leave, probably happy in the knowledge that his wife was pregnant with their first child. The past four weeks had also been quiet for him, only achieving two victories between the 16th of September and the 17th of October.* However, he must have been pleased with himself for as well as looking forwards to being a father, his thirty-first kill on the 12th of October was the 500th kill for the whole Gruppe making it even more a reason for celebration. He had now been in near continuous action for over a year and, it is likely that the strains of this and the responsibility of leading the Gruppe were beginning to tell.

Meanwhile, over London, *3 Staffel* had dropped their bombs and were flying east, headed for home. When, over the Thames Estuary, the inevitable happened and the formation was bounced by RAF fighters.

---

* His daughter Hanne-Birgit Mayer was born on 2 July 1941 – *Author*

Oberleutnant Walter Rupp's fighter was hit by a burst of fire, (probably by Pilot Officer Bryan Draper of 74 Squadron) and his *Rottenflieger, Fähnrich* Walter Seiz, reported that Rupp's aircraft was losing coolant from the engine. Walter Rupp immediately turned for France but, with his engine overheating rapidly, he knew that this was impossible and faced either a ditching in the Channel with the hope that he would be picked up by the German air sea rescue or force-landing in enemy territory. Spotting the airfield of Manston, he chose the latter option but, just before landing, remembered that he was carrying new types of ammunition. He fired all his guns, much to the alarm of the airfield personnel, as his fighter landed on its belly and slithered to a stop. Before his inevitable capture, he fired his pistol at the instrument panel and then handed his gun to the first officer that approached his aircraft.

Oblt *Prestelle in the cockpit of his 'Red 2', Le Touquet, October 1940*

Hanne-Birgit Mayer, daughter of Hans Karl Mayer, born 2 July 1941, is in the cot presented to her by JG 53

Oberleutnant Ignatz Prestelle was also experiencing a few technical problems with his fighter and radioed that he was going to turn back. With two of the three Staffel leaders, one of which was also leading the Gruppe, now out of commission, and the remaining fighters heavily engaged in combat, the situation looked desperate for *Oberleutnant* Hans Ohly who was now forced to lead the whole Gruppe.

As this drama was unfolding Hans-Karl Mayer, back at the airfield at Etaples, had taken off to test fly a new Messerschmitt Bf 109E-7. It is thought that soon after take off, Mayer heard over the radio that his Gruppe was in trouble and took it upon himself to fly to their aid. He was last seen crossing the coast but never made it to where his Gruppe were fighting. Nothing further was heard from him over the radio and it was later learnt that his aircraft carried no ammunition and, more importantly, no one-man dinghy.

Ten days later a body was washed ashore at Littlestone in Kent, it was collected by personnel from the nearby RAF airfield of Hawkinge and taken to the Station mortuary. This German airman, as it turned out, carried no form of identification or personal effects apart from an identity disc numbered 67005/1. With no further clues, the body was buried in the cemetery just behind the airfield on the 1st of November as an 'Unknown German Airman'.

The finding of the body was reported to RAF Intelligence who were also

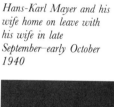

Hans-Karl Mayer and his wife home on leave with his wife in late September−early October 1940

sent the identity disc and number. The personnel in the AI 1(k) Department, who being used to such mysteries, soon realised that the body was that of *Hauptmann* Mayer. Squadron Leader S D Felkin, head of the Department, wrote the following in his report:

> The identity disc number 67005/1 is that of 1/JG 53 but this officer was the *Gruppenkommandeur* of I/JG 53. He is thought to have been previously the *Staffelkapitän* of the *1st Staffel* and this is no doubt where he got his identity disc. His position as *Staffelkapitän* is confirmed by the individual number '1' on the disc.
>
> From interrogation it has been ascertained that he failed to return from a war flight about three weeks ago. The exact date is not known. *Hauptmann* MAYER was a promising officer who had received rapid promotion. He fought in Spain with the Condor Legion and had won several medals. In September last, when he claimed twenty victories, he was awarded the Knight's Cross.

The Gruppenkommandeur's brand new 'Emil' – October 1940

Hans-Karl Mayer – born 9 March 1911 . . .

. . . Died 17 October 1940; his grave at Hawkinge in Kent (his name is mis-spelt as is the date of his death)

A simple cross was placed on his grave which said HAUPTMANN MAYER – 27 OCTOBER 1940. His Geschwader soon learned that he was dead but it was not until the late 1980's that the survivors from *I Gruppe* knew where he lay. In 1990 two of his *Staffelkapitäne*, Hans Ohly and Walter Rupp, were able to pay their last respects to their friend but even today, the exact reasons for his death are not known.*

The loss of Hans-Karl Mayer came as a great shock to the whole Geschwader. He had managed, so far during the war, to survive without injury to himself and now, to have been lost under unknown circumstances, was incomprehensible and affected the morale of all those who had flown with him and had been under his command. Even today, he is still talked about with great affection by those who knew him and these sentiments are best summed up by Werner Karl:

> To me, *Hauptmann* Mayer was the most remarkable personality, he was exemplary in every respect. I remember him especially for two reasons. Firstly, he was so tall, he used to cram himself into his cockpit and when on missions used twice as much oxygen than the rest of us. Secondly, I remember one combat he fought with me as his *Rottenflieger*. He had just shot down an RAF fighter, I cannot remember the date or whether it was a Spitfire or Hurricane. The British pilot had baled out and *Hauptmann* Mayer was genuinely happy that the pilot had escaped. However, as I watched the pilot descend, I saw an orange glow getting bigger and bigger – the parachute was on fire and soon collapsed and the British pilot fell to his death. On landing, I told *Hauptmann* Mayer what he had not seen and he was genuinely upset.

Command of the Gruppe was now given temporarily to *Oberleutnant* Ignatz Prestelle until *Hauptmann* Hans-Heinrich Brüstellin was posted in from I/JG 51. Although an experienced pilot himself, having commanded I/JG 51 from September 1939, Brüstellin only had four victories so far in the war and he must have had a hard task taking over from a very popular *Gruppenkommandeur* who had amassed, by the time of his death, a total of thirty one victories (as well as an additional eight victories from the Spanish Civil War).

The remainder of October 1940 was very much an anti-climax. *Oberleutnant* Hans Ohly records a further eleven operational flights which on each occasion were escort flights for 3/JG 53, that Staffel now being commanded by *Oberleutnant* Werner Ursinus, the former Adjutant of II/JG 53. In each case, no combats were fought and *I Gruppe* did not increase its score of five hundred victories until the 22nd of June 1941.** Likewise the Staffel and Gruppe did not lose any of their fighters in combat for the

---

* After the war, a head stone was placed over the grave, inscribed HANS CARL MAYER – BORN 9 MARCH 1911, DIED 27 OCTOBER 1940. The German War Graves Commission are considering changing the head stone to give the correct spelling of his name and date of death – *Author*

** The 22nd of June 1941 was the first day of Operation *Barbarossa*, the German invasion of the Soviet Union. The first victory for I/JG 53 for over eight months went to a *1 Staffel* pilot – *Unteroffizier* Ludwig Reibel – *Author*

remainder of the month and the only item of note was that Hans Ohly's beloved Messerschmitt Bf 109 coded 'White 7' began to suffer increasing engine problems necessitating an engine change and him flying 'White 5' until 'White 7' was returned to him later in November 1940.

As Autumn ended and Winter commenced, the tempo for 1 Staffel did not change but some of the missions did. For instance, during the afternoon of the 1st of November 1940, the Luftwaffe's Stukas made an appearance over the Channel for the first time since the 18th of August 1940 when they had carried out attacks against the airfields in and around the Solent with disastrous results for many of their crews. During two attacks against shipping in the Thames Estuary and Dover Straits, apparently by *Major Paul Hozzel's I/StG 1*, the only victories against the RAF were claimed by *Oberstleutnant* Adolf Galland's JG 26 whilst *1 Staffel* and the remainder of JG 53 returned without incident.

As the month progressed missions ranged from the usual escort sorties for *3 Staffel* and reconnaissance, by a Henschel Hs 126 spotter plane, to two *Freie Jagd* missions. The second mission, on the 16th of November, resulting in one of the new pilots, *Fähnrich* Wolfgang Hauffe crashing landing back at Etaples. In all November 1940 was a dull month for *1 Staffel*, the typical poor winter weather being the victor. All that the pilots could write in their log books for each mission was *Ohne Luftkampf*, 'without air battle'.

JG 53 celebrates over 2000 missions. Left to right: Lt *Schultz (1/JG 53),* Oblt *Brändle (4/JG 53),* Hptm *Wilcke (Kdr III/JG 53),* Major *von Maltzahn (Geschwader Kommodore),* Hptm *Bretnütz (Kdr II/JG 53),* Ofw *Litjens (4/JG 53),* Hptm *Brüstellin (Kdr I/JG 53),* Lt *Schiess (Stab/JG 53),* Oblt *Götz (StKap 9/JG 53), France, October 1940*

Understandably the pilots of the Staffel were, by now, becoming tired of continual operations over the Channel without incident. The first flight of December 1940, a seventy-five minute *Freie Jagd* over the Channel, with *Oberleutnant* Hans Ohly leading the Gruppe, was exactly the same as the November missions, *Ohne Luftkampf.* However, the following day was different.

Around lunch time on the 2nd of December 1940, the Staffel took off on a *Freie Jagd.* Hans Ohly did not fly on this mission and it is not known who commanded the Staffel but the objective of the *Freie Jagd,* to draw up the RAF fighters, was achieved with fatal consequences for one of the *1 Staffel* pilots. The RAF Squadron that intercepted them was 74 Squadron, commanded by Squadron Leader Adolph 'Sailor' Malan, a particularly successful and aggressive Spitfire squadron. One of the RAF pilots flying this day was Sergeant John Glendinning who reported the following events on returning to 74 Squadron's base at Biggin Hill:

> We were told to patrol Maidstone at Angels 25,000 plus. We climbed to this height and heard my Squadron Leader tell Yellow Section to break away and attack. I was still following my Section Leader who then broke away into a dive as an Me 109 went past his nose, or so it appeared to me. I followed him down and was circling around when I perceived an Me 109 about to close in and do a 'beam' attack. I allowed two wings for deflection and fired a few seconds burst into him; he went immediately straight into a spin and what appeared to be black oil and glycol was pouring from him as he went down. I broke away and looked around to see if there was anything else. I

Wing Commander 'Sailor' Malan, formerly of 74 Squadron, talks tactics with Wing Commander Michael Robinson, formerly of 609 Squadron

then heard my Section Leader calling for Blue Section to reform; this I did and climbed with my Section back to 27,000 feet to intercept a further eighteen plus raid of Me 109s. Through this I was unable to find out the ultimate fate of the Me 109 I fired on.

Although Glendinning and another two pilots, Pilot Officer Harbourne Stephen and Sergeant Neil Morrison claimed a German fighter as 'probably' destroyed and Flying Officer Henryk Szczsny claimed one as 'damaged', only 'Sailor' Malan was credited with a Messerschmitt Bf 109 'destroyed' when he sent one into the Channel off Dungeness at 1224 hours. His victim was twenty-two year old *Leutnant* Siegfried Fischer whose fighter was last seen near Dungeness. Siegfried Fischer had joined *1 Staffel* from *3 Staffel* in September as a replacement for one of the pilots lost during that month. He himself was an experienced fighter pilot, having claimed his first victory over France on the 13th of May 1940, and his fifth and last,

Sergeant John Glendinning

Lt *Siegfried Fischer*

(on the 15th of September 1940), shortly before joining *1 Staffel*. Again, he was a popular pilot with an infectious smile who was sadly missed by his fellow pilots.

Interestingly, as 74 Squadron returned to Biggin Hill, the British 'Y' Service, which was manned by personnel who monitored German radio transmissions, heard that one German fighter, Siegfried Fischer's, had crashed in the Channel off Dungeness at 1227 hours and that another German fighter was in difficulties. This aircraft was reported to have crashed mid-Channel at 1246 hours and shortly afterwards its pilot was rescued. This second aircraft turned out to be that flown by *Fähnrich* Wolfgang Hauffe and one of the 'probables' claimed by 74 Squadron could now be upgraded to a 'destroyed'.

The weather now made operational flights, for *1 Staffel*, few and far between and when the Geschwader was told that it would be returning to Germany for a rest on the 19th of December, the pilots must have breathed a sigh of relief. Unfortunately, the Staffel was to suffer one more loss before the end of 1940. On the 11th of December the whole Geschwader was tasked with a *Freie Jagd* and *Jabo* escort sortie which was in fact to be the last operational flight flown by JG 53 for 1940. The Geschwader was not to increase its total victories on this mission as no combats were fought. However, for one of the *1 Staffel* pilots, a well deserved rest in Germany was not to be.

1 Staffel, again flying without their *Staffelkapitän*, was tasked with escorting the *Jabos* of *3 Staffel* to an unspecified target in the London area. The flight was uneventful but on the return, the fighter flown by *Unteroffizier* Rudi Müller was seen to peel away and, for no obvious reason, dive into the cloud. Free from their escort duty, the Staffel went to find out what had happened but all that they could find was a green patch on the surface of

The lucky ones: pilots from JG 53, now prisoners of War, pose for the families back in Germany, Canada, Sep/Oct 43:
Standing, Left to right:
?, Fw Xaver Ray (8/JG 53, POW 2 Nov 40), Uffz Hans Schulte (7/JG 53, POW 6 Sep 40), Fw Christian Hansen (2/JG 53, POW 16 Aug 40), ?, Fw Anton Ochsenkühn (9/ JG 53, POW 5 Sep 40), Uffz Willi Ghesla (1/JG 53, POW 5 Oct 40), Gefr Josef Bröker (1/JG 53, POW 25 Aug 40)
Front, Left to right:
Uffz Gerd Beitz (9/JG 53, POW 18 May 42), Fw Herbert Tzschoppe (1/JG 53, POW 15 Sep 40), Fw Heinrich Höhnisch (1/JG 53, POW 9 Sep 40), Ofw Franz Kaiser (1/JG 53, POW 22 Apr 42), Fw Walter Scholz (3/JG 53, POW Sep 40), Uffz Karl Heinz Feldmann (3/JG 53, POW 15 Sep 40), Uffz Werner Karl (1/JG 53, POW 2 Sep 40)

the sea directly below where Rudi Müller had last been seen. The weather conditions at time were not at all good and it was assumed that Müller's fighter had become iced up and he had lost control. However, as the Staffel was at that time flying at 4,000 metres, this would have given him plenty of time to either regain control and get out of his Messerschmitt before it hit the Channel. The true cause of his death will never be known. Twenty-two year old Rudi Müller had only joined the Staffel in October 1940 and in his short career as a fighter pilot had failed to gain any victories.

This was a sad note on which *1 Staffel* would finish the Battle of Britain, 1940 and their part in this book. Eight days later, having flown no further operational flights, JG 53 began to fly back to Germany for rest and recuperation and early in the new year, traded its battle weary Messerschmitt Bf 109Es for the newer F or *'Friedrich'* version. At 1725 hours *1 Staffel* lifted off from Etaples for the last time and headed for Krefeld in Germany. As with many of the flights flown by *1 Staffel* towards the end of 1940 it was the weather that had the last word. Deteriorating conditions forced the Staffel to divert to the airfield at Mauberge on the French-Belgian border and it eventually arrived back in Germany twenty four hours later. *1 Staffel* was not to return to France until the 2nd of April 1941 when it would find itself flying against an RAF that was now using totally different tactics and, furthermore, was determined to bring the battle to the Luftwaffe whose pilots found themselves flying more and more defensive missions. The battle for Britain was well and truly finished for 1/JG 53.

CHAPTER ELEVEN

Postscript

The months that JG 53 were based on the Channel Coast during the first half of 1941 were much quieter in comparison to the previous Summer. Between the 19th of March and the 4th of June 1941, the Geschwader claimed twenty-seven victories but none of them were claimed by *1 Staffel* or, for that matter, by *I Gruppe*. During that time, only two aircraft from the Geschwader were lost in combat with one pilot being killed, the other becoming a prisoner of war.

609 Squadron moved from Warmwell to Biggin Hill in Kent on the 24th of February 1941 and were destined to face 1/JG 53 for the first time since the end of August 1940. During the period 24th of February to the 4th of June 1941 (the later date being the date that 1/JG 53 was withdrawn from the Channel Front in preparation for the invasion of the Soviet Union), 609 Squadron was far more successful than the German Staffel, claiming eleven confirmed victories for the loss of five pilots.

It cannot be positively confirmed whether 609 Squadron did meet 1/ JG 53 in combat during 1941. However, on the very day that 1/JG 53 was withdrawn from the Channel Coast, a pilot who had only recently been transferred from 1/JG 53 and who had fought against 609 Squadron ten months earlier, met a 609 Squadron pilot who had also fought against 1/ JG 53 during the previous Summer. For both pilots, the results would be tragic.

By the 4th of June 1941, 609 Squadron had settled in to operating out of Biggin Hill and were using the new tactics instigated by Fighter Command. At 1640 hours on this day the Squadron, together with Spitfires from 92 Squadron, took off to escort six Blenheims who were to attack cargo ships off Boulogne. The Squadron noted with annoyance that the Blenheims failed to drop their bombs and that they had to suffer being shot at by the Boulogne anti-aircraft guns. Despite the anti-aircraft fire, all the RAF aircraft returned undamaged.

At 1615 hours, shortly before 609 Squadron took off, 4/JG 53 was scrambled to intercept RAF aircraft detected off the French Coast and soon the German fighters became involved in combat with Spitfires from 54 Squadron. Flying Officer George Gribble DFC, an experienced and popular pilot who had flown during the Dunkirk Evacuation and the Battle of Britain, was lost during this combat. Some records say his aircraft suffered engine failure but, at the time he was lost, *Feldwebel* Stephan Litjens of 4/ JG 53 claimed to have shot down a Spitfire, the German pilot's seventh kill. George Gribble was seen to bale out ten miles south of Dover and, as a result, an air sea rescue search was started for him.

At 1926 hours 609 Squadron took off to escort a Westland Lysander searching for George Gribble. Four of 609's Spitfires flew to Hawkinge to escort another Lysander on the same mission, leaving nine aircraft to patrol in two sections at 2,000 feet off Dover. As the formation flew to and fro they spotted a rescue launch and the two Lysanders hunting for the downed pilot. Suddenly they spotted three Messerschmitt Bf 109s streaking towards the Lysanders 1,000 feet below them. These were three aircraft from the *Stabschwarm* of JG 53 – *Major* Günther von Maltzahn, *Kommodore* of *Jagdgeschwader 53*, who together with *Leutnant* Franz Schiess and *Feldwebel* Heinrich Rühl had seen the air sea rescue aircraft and was intent on making what was to be JG 53's last flight over the Channel, before being withdrawn, a successful one.

Feldwebel Heinrich Rühl had flown with 1/JG 53 throughout the Battle of Britain and had scored five victories but on the 16th of May 1941 he had been transferred from his Staffel to fly with the Geschwader's *Kommodore* in the *Stabschwarm* – a great honour. It was also an honour to be flying on the Geschwader's last mission before leaving the Channel Coast and this could have accounted for Rühl's eagerness to get one more Spitfire before leaving. What happened next is best described by the 609 Squadron Intelligence Officer, Flying Officer Frank Ziegler, who wrote the following after 609's Spitfires returned:

Oblt Hans Ohly in his brand new 'Friedrich'

The last known photo of Herbert Rühl (front row, second from left) with other pilots from 1/JG 53, April 1941. Back row left to right: Lt Zellot, Uffz Bubenzer, Lt Schultz, Oblt Ohly, Lt Hauffe, Lt Padior. Front, Gefr Pielach, Fw Rühl, Ofw Schäfer, Uffz Reibel. Taken at Crécy nr. Abbeville, France

Flight Lieutenant Johnnie Curchin DFC (centre) flanked by Flying Officer Hal Tidswell (Adjutant) and Pilot Officer Sidney Hill

First comes Pilot Officer de Spirlet with a faulty oil gauge – he has nothing to relate. The other pilots arrive in driblets which presupposes action. The Commanding Officer (Squadron Leader Robinson) taxies up with gun canvasses shot away and emerges from his plane sweating. He has fought for at least ten minutes, he says, and is obviously tired. He thinks he has got one – he saw a splash but, before that, he saw a Spitfire go in. The Sergeant Rigler appears, all cock-a-hoop; he has got one – no doubt about that – and probably another (all very difficult for, of the three, one, says the CO returned to France). Next comes Pilot Officer Ortmanns 'Yes, I fire' he laughs 'but the Jerry he goes in' (thank goodness he does not make a claim). Suddenly, pilots stop arriving and there are still five more missing. Everyone seems to be certain that one 109 and one Spit has gone into the drink. The latter, we speculate, must be either Sergeant Boyd or Pilot Officer van Lierde – both Number Fours. Four aircraft are reported at Hawkinge and West Malling. Momentarily there is a rumour of another at Manston. Momentarily, the CO smiles and everybody smiles for it seems that after all we have lot no one and the Spit was another 109. Boyd and van Lierde both come in. Then it suddenly dawns on us that the most unbelievable; the missing pilot is Johnie – Johnie Curchin.

Flight Lieutenant John Curchin had taken command of 'B' Flight in April 1941. He had fought with the Squadron throughout the Battle of Britain and was a wild and popular member of the Squadron and Flight Commander. He had scored nine victories by June 1941 and had been awarded the DFC back in November 1940. The events of this encounter recorded by both sides; one of the German pilots saw a Messerschmitt Bf 109 attack the Spitfires and believed that it had collided with one of the enemy fighters. 609 Squadron's account was written in the Intelligence Report by Frank Ziegler and submitted to Group Headquarters. The following is part of that report:

> Blue Two, Pilot Officer Mackenzie, reports an enemy aircraft which shot between him and his leader, Flight Lieutenant Curchin DFC, and it seems probable that this was the aircraft that shot the latter down. Outside witnesses confirm that a Spitfire went into the sea, and the pilot evidently was unable to bale out.

As no claims were submitted by the other two German pilots involved, it is assumed that Heinrich Rühl got his sixth victory but lost his life in doing so. Neither he or John Curchin were ever seen again. 609 Squadron and JG 53 had met for the last time.

CHAPTER 12

Brothers in Arms?

For both 609 Squadron and 1/JG 53 the war was by no means over. 609
Squadron was destined to be in the RAF's front line for virtually all of the
war, flying interceptions and sweeps from Biggin Hill and Gravesend in
1941, then in 1942 replacing their Spitfires with the new Hawker Typhoon
fighter. With these new aircraft the Squadron was soon to become the
premier Typhoon squadron and continued to fly them even when the
Squadron's role changed from a fighter to a ground attack unit. The
Squadron was heavily involved in the invasion of Normandy and took part
in the campaigns in France, Belgium and eventually Germany, flying its
last operational mission on the 4th of May 1945.

1/JG 53 was also in the Luftwaffe's front line for the remainder of the
war. It was to fly in Russia and over Malta in 1941, Russia and Malta and
Tunisia in 1942, Tunisia, Sicily, Italy in 1943 and Italy, Rumania and
Hungary in 1944. *1 Staffel* was to end its war flying in Hungary and scored
its last confirmed kill, a Russian Lavochkin 7 fighter shot down by *Leutnant*
Arno Fischer, on the 9th of April 1945.

Both the RAF and Luftwaffe units had been operational from the first
to the last day of the war. During the period covered by this book, 609
Squadron scored eighty-eight confirmed air combat victories and lost six
pilots killed or missing. 1/JG 53 scored fifty-one confirmed victories and
with seven pilots being made prisoners of war and three killed or missing.

Heaving read the preceding chapters and learned how each side fought,
survived and in some cases died, can the reader say that the fighter pilots,
from these two nationalities, be regarded as a sort of 'brothers in arms'?
What must be borne in mind when thinking about this is that one cannot
ignore that the Luftwaffe was an instrument which tried to further Adolf
Hitler's National Socialist aims and ideals therefore, in the true sense of the
phrase, the answer must be no. However, take away politics and a dictator,
both fighter units were doing a job. One was defending its country, the
other defending aircraft flown by fellow countrymen as well as being a true
fighter unit and fighting against the aircraft of an enemy nation in a fight
of life and death. This can best be summed up by the views of some of the
surviving pilots. For many, on both sides, it was the machine not the man
that they were after, as illustrated by what one 609 Squadron pilot said
recently:

> When we were up there, it was not the pilot that we were after but the
> aircraft. If the pilot got out, I was always pleased to see his parachute open.

On the subject of politics, most German pilots did not discuss Hitler and the Nazi party, preferring to discuss fighting, flying and staying alive. However, one *1 Staffel* pilot, when asked did any one talk about politics, said:

> Yes. I was surprised how critically some officers commented about our military (especially Hermann Goering) and political leadership.

The 1990's has seen or will see the fiftieth anniversaries of incidents that happened during all but the first few months of the Second World War. Understandably, these anniversaries have brought back many memories, some good, many bad and have reopened many wounds long since thought to be healed. There will be some who read this book who, for personal reasons, disagree strongly that Luftwaffe and RAF fighter pilots could ever be regarded as 'brothers in arms' and as a historian, I can understand and respect their sentiments. However, if I have shown that today it can be said that there is a sort of bond between the pilots of 609 Squadron and the pilots of 1/JG 53 formed by the fear of being shot down, the sadness of losing a fellow pilot, elation at surviving and a basic love of flying fighter aircraft, I hope that those who disagree with the term 'brothers in arms' will understand why this book has been written.

Hans Ohly and Hans Karl Mayer

Keith Ogilvie and 'Teeny' Overton

RAF & Luftwaffe Claims and Losses for the Attack on Warmwell, 25 August 1940

RAF Claims

Sqn	Pilot	Details
17	Sqn Ldr C W Williams	Bf 110 damaged, 1650 hrs
	Plt Off P E Pitman	Bf 110 destroyed, Bf 110 damaged off Portland
	Fg Off M B Czernin	3 Bf 110s destroyed (first 2 ac crashed in the sea, 3rd ac crashed 2 miles SE of Dorchester, one crew member baling out; this ac also attacked by 2 Spitfires)
	Pt Off D W H Hanson	Bf 109 probable, Bf 110 probable
	Flt Lt A W Bayne	2 Bf 110s probable (one shared with Plt Off D H Wissler)
	Plt Off H A C Bird-Wilson	Bf 110 destroyed 30 miles south of Weymouth
	Plt Off D C Leary	Bf 109 destroyed near Warmwell
	Sgt D A Sewell	Bf 109 probable
87	Wg Cdr J S Dewar	Ju 88 destroyed, Bf 109 probable
	Flt Ltr I R Gleed	Bf 110 destroyed, Bf 110 probable, Bf 109 damaged
	Fg Off W D David	Ju 88 destroyed, Bf 109 destroyed 3 miles NW Portland
	Plt Off H J Mitchell	Bf 109 destroyed over sea
	Plt Off R P Beamont	Bf 109 destroyed Buckland Ripers, Do 17 damaged
	Fg Off K W Tait	Bf 109 destroyed off Chesil Bank, Bf 110 destroyed at sea
	Fg Off R W Watson	Bf 109 damaged
	Sgt I J Badger	Ju 88 probable, Bf 109 damaged
	Fg Off R F G Malengreau	Ju 88 damaged
	Sgt F Howell	Bf 109 probable
	Sgt L A Thorogood	Ju 88 destroyed
152	Plt Off E S Marrs	Bf 110 destroyed
	Sgt J K Barker	Bf 109 destroyed over sea
	Plt Off W Beaumont	Bf 109 destroyed, Buckland Ripers
	Flt Lt F M Thomas	Ju 88 probable
213	Sgt R T Llewellyn	Bf 109 destroyed, Buckland Ripers, Bf 110 destroyed
	Sgt E G Snowden	Ju 88 off Swyre
	Fg Off J M Strickland	Bf 109 over sea, Bf 110 damaged?
	Plt Off J A L Philippart?	Bf 109 destroyed
	?	Bf 110 damaged
602	Sgt C Babbage	Bf 110 destroyed, Do 17 destroyed over sea
	Flt Lt R F Boyd	2 Bf 109s destroyed 3 miles south of Seaton

	Fg Off D McF Jack	½ Bf 110 destroyed (shared with Sgt Elcombe)
	Sgt D W Elcombe	½ Bf 110 destroyed (shared with Fg Off Jack)
	Plt Off T G F Ritchie	Bf 110 destroyed
	Fg Off P C Webb	Bf 110 destroyed over sea, Bf 110 destroyed at Winfrith
	Sqn Ldr A V R Johnstone	Bf 110 destroyed, Bf 109 destroyed
	?	Do 17 destroyed
	?	Do 17 destroyed
	?	Bf 109 damaged
609	Sqn Ldr H S Darley	Bf 110 destroyed, Bf 109 destroyed 2 miles south of Warmwell
	Flt Lt F J Howell	Bf 110 destroyed
	Flt Lt J H G McArthur	Bf 110 destroyed between Warmwell & Poole
	Fg Off J C Dundas	Bf 110 probable
	Plt Off J Curchin	Bf 109 destroyed (exploded)
	Plt Off E Q Tobin	Bf 110 probable, Bf 110 damaged
	Plt Off G Gaunt	½ Bf 110 destroyed Wareham (shared with Plt Off Agazarian)
	Plt Off N Le C Agazarian	½ Bf 110 destroyed Wareham (shared with Plt Off Gaunt)
	Sgt A N Feary	Bf 110 destroyed, Bf 110 damaged

Luftwaffe Claims

Unit	Pilot	Details
Stab/JG 2	*Maj* W Schellmann	Spitfire near Warmwell, 1730 hrs
3/JG 2	*Uffz* F Stritzel	Spitfire
3/JG 2	*Oblt* H Wick	One Spitfire, one Hurricane
4/JG 2	*Oblt* H Hahn	Spitfire, Dorchester
5/JG 2	*Oblt* F Bölz	Spitfire, 1735 hrs
8/JG 2	*Oblt* K-H Metz	Hurricane near Portland, 1735 hrs
9/JG 2	*Oblt* C Röders	Hurricane near Weymouth, 1734 hrs
7/JG 27	*Fw* E Clade	Spitfire near Portland, 1742 hrs
7/JG 27	*Oblt* L Franzisket	Hurricane near Portland, 1755 hrs
7/JG 27	*Oblt* K Fischer	Hurricane near Portland
1/JG 53		Seven Hurricanes (see Appendix F)
3/JG 53	*Fw* W Schölz	One
	Lt S Fischer	One
4/JG 53	*Oblt* G Schulze-Blanck	Hurricane, 1708 hrs
7/JG 53	*Fw* H Neuhoff	Spitfire, unconfirmed
8/JG 53	*Hptm* H von Hahn	Spitfire
	Oblt H Kunert	Spitfire, 1829 hrs
9/JG 53	*Lt* J Stoll	Spitfire, 1836 hrs
I/ZG 2		Three Spitfires
II/ZG 2		One Hurricane
III/ZG 76		Five
V(Z)/LG 1		Two
15(Z)/LG 1	*Lt* R Altendorf	Hurricane, south of the Isle of Wight
I/KG 51		One

RAF Losses

Sqn	Aircraft	Pilot	Details
17	Hurricane R4199	Sqn Ldr C W Williams	Pilot missing – port wing shot off by Bf 110, ac spun into sea near Portland, 1720 hrs
	Hurricane V7407	Flt Lt S Q Bayne	Pilot uninjured – shot down in combat, pilot baled out near Portlane, 1725 hrs
87	Hurricane V7250	Sgt R E Wakeling	Pilot killed – crashed at New Barn, Dorchester
152	Spitfire R6994	Plt Off R M Hogg	Pilot missing – near Portland, 1715 hrs
	Spitfire R6810	Plt Off T S Wildblood	Pilot missing – near Portland
213	Hurricane P2766	Plt Off H D Atkinson DFC	Pilot killed – shot down near Portland, 1730 hrs; pilot's body washed ashore later
	Hurricane W6668/AK-I	Plt Off J A L Philippart	Pilot killed – shot down near Portland; pilot's body washed ashore at Weymouth
	Hurricane N2646	Sgt E G Snowden	Pilot uninjured – force-landed near Burton Bradstock after combat
	Hurricane P3200	Plt Off H D Clark	Pilot wounded – ac damaged in combat (possibly shot down off Portland; pilot admitted to Weymouth Hospital)
	Hurricane V7226	Unknown	Pilot uninjured – ac damaged in combat
602	Spitfire N3226	Sgt M H Sprague	Pilot uninjured – shot down near Portland, pilot baled out
	Spitfire P9381	Plt Off W H Coverley	Pilot uninjured – crashed at Galton Heath, pilot baled out
609	Spitfire R6986	Fg Off P Ostazewski-Ostoja	Pilot slightly wounded – ac damaged in combat and crashed on landing at Warmwell; ac written off
	Spitfire R6961	Plt Off D M Crook	Pilot uninjured – ac damaged in combat with Bf 110

Luftwaffe losses

Unit	Aircraft	Pilot	Details
III/JG 2	Bf 109E-1	Unknown	Pilot rescued – ditched in Channel following combat
	Bf 109E-1	Unknown	Pilot rescued – ditched in Channel following combat
	Bf 109E-1	Unknown	Pilot uninjured – crashed on landing due to combat damage
1/JG 53	Bf 109E-1, White 15	*Gefr* J Bröker	Pilot wounded (POW) – shot down in combat with Spitfire of 152 Sqn, Hurricanes of 87 & 213 Sqns. Crash-landed at Buckland Ripers, Dorset, 1732 hrs
6/JG 53	Bf 109E-4	*Hptm* A Maculan	Pilot missing – probably claimed by Sqn Ldr Darley, 609 Sqn & Fg Off Tait of 87 Sqn. Crashed into sea just off Chesil Bank
	Bf 109E-4	*Ofw* A Baun	Pilot rescued but wounded – shot down 15 miles SW of Portland, 1745 hrs
	Bf 109E-4	*Fw* B Seufert	Pilot rescued but wounded – shot down off Weymouth
	Bf 109E	*Fw* W Margstein	Pilot rescued but wounded – shot down SW of Portland

| 13/LG 1 | Bf 110C-2 | *Oblt* J Glienke | Pilot missing – near Warmwell |
| | | *Uffz* P Stuck | R/Op missing |

14/LG 1	Bf 110C-2	*Fw* K Rohrung	Pilot uninjured
		Ogefr H Grosse	R/Op wounded – ac belly-landed at Roquancourt and written-off
	Bf 110C-2,	*Uffz* A Pfaffelhuber	Pilot uninjured
	L1+NL	*Uffz* W Banser (?)	R/Op uninjured
			Crash-landed at Barfleur

15/LG 1	Bf 110C-4	*Uffz* H Hamann	Pilot (POW)
		Uffz W Maresch	R/Op missing
			Shot down off Warmwell

| I/ZG 2 | Bf 110C-4 | Unknown | Crew unhurt – suffered 20% damage in combat |

1/ZG 2	Bf 110C-2,	*Oblt* G Götz	Pilot (POW)
	3M+AH	*Uffz* K Haupt	R/Op (POW)
			Shot down by Sgt Feary, 609 Sqn & crashed at Creech Barrow, Wareham, 1745 hrs
	Bf 110C-4,	*Lt* K Westphal	Pilot killed
	3M+CH,	*Uffz* J Brief	R/Op killed
	2123?		Shot down by Fg Off Webb, 602 Sqn & exploded over Maryfield, Winfrith, Dorset, 1800 hrs
	Bf 110C-4,	*Uffz* S Becker	Pilot (POW)
	3M+KH,	*Ogefr* W Wötzel	R/Op (POW)
	3208?		Shot down by Plt Off Gaunt & Plt Off Agazarian, 609 Sqn & crashed at East Holme, Wareham, 1800 hrs
	Bf 110C-4	*Uffz* K Hörner	Pilot missing
		Uffz G Kirsch	R/Op missing
			Missing near Warmwell

II/ZG 2	Bf 110C-4	Crew unhurt	Suffered 25% combat damage
	Bf 110C-4	Crew unhurt	Written off after combat
	Bf 110D-0	Crew unhurt	Suffered 20% combat damage

8/ZG 76	Bf 110C-4,	*Fw* M Dähne	Pilot missing
	2728	*Ogefr* F Müller	R/Op missing
			Possibly shot down by Flt Lt McArthur of 609 Sqn and crashed at Symond's Farm, Buckland Ripers, Dorset, 1730 hrs

II/KG 51	Ju 88A-1	*Lt* E Bender	Pilot wounded
		Sd Fhr H Grosse	Wounded
		2 other crew	Uninjured
			Ditched 30 kms north of Cherbourg after combat

6/KG 51	Ju 88A-1	*Uffz* G Hansen	Pilot missing
		Uffz K Kipping	Obs missing
		Ogefr D Brabdt	R/Op missing
		Flg J Meidinger	AG missing
			Shot down off Portland

609 Squadron Pilots – August–December 1940

Name	Service No	Details
Squadron Leader H S Darley	32191	Squadron Commander until 4 Oct 40; awarded DSO 9 Oct 40. Survived war.
Squadron Leader M L Robinson	37300	Posted to command Sqn 4 Oct 40; awarded DFC 17 Nov 40. Later awarded DSO. Reported missing in combat near Le Touquet 10 Apr 42 as Wg Cdr Leader, Tangmere Wg whilst flying Spitfire W3770.
Flight Lieutenant S G Beaumont	90319	On Sqn Aug 40 as B Flight Commander. Posted away 2 Aug 40. Later awarded OBE. Survived war.
Flight Lieutenant J C Dundas	90334	On Sqn Aug 40, promoted to command B Flight Sep 40. Awarded DFC 20 Oct 40 but reported missing in combat 28 Nov 40; awarded posthumous Bar to DFC.
Flight Lieutenant T H T Forshaw	39165	Joined Sqn 9 Sep 40. Promoted to command B Flight No 40. Survived war.
Flight Lieutenant F J Howell	39612	On Sqn Aug 40 as A Flight Commander; awarded DFC 25 Oct 40. Later awarded Bar to DFC. Killed in accident post-war.
Flight Lieutenant J H G McArthur	37925	Posted in early Aug 40 to be B Flight Commander. Posted away Sep 40 and awarded DFC for work with 609 Sqn. Killed in flying accident post-war.
Flying Officer J D Bisdee	76575	On Sqn Aug 40; later awarded DFC & survived war.
Flying Officer A R Edge	90325	On Sqn Aug 40; posted from Sqn Aug 40. Later awarded AFC & survived war.
Flying Officer H McC Goodwin	90269	On Sqn Aug 40. Killed in action while with Sqn 14 Aug 40.
Flying Officer E L Hancock	70278	Joined Sqn 25 Sep 40. Later awarded DFC & survived war.
Flying Officer B W Little	90326	On Sqn Aug 40. Posted away Aug 40. Later awarded OBE. Survived war.
Flying Officer J C Newbery	70497	On Sqn Aug 40. Posted Dec 40 & survived war.
Flying Officer T Nowierski	76803	Joined Sqn Aug 40. Later awarded DFC & survived war.
Flying Officer P Ostaszewski-Ostoja	76741	Joined Sqn Aug 40. Survived war.
Flying Officer C N Overton	40639	On Sqn Aug 40. Later awarded DFC & survived war.
Pilot Officer N Le C Agazarian	72550	On Sqn Aug 40. Killed in action near Gambut, Libya on 16 May 41 whilst flying in Hurricane W9302 of 274 Sqn.
Pilot Officer M J Appleby	90962	On Sqn Aug 40; posted Oct 40. Survived war.
Pilot Officer J A Atkinson	83676	Joined Sqn 29 Nov 40. Later awarded DFC and survived war.
Pilot Officer P A Baillon	86331	Joined Sqn 29 Sep 40. Killed in action while with Sqn 28 Nov 40.

Pilot Officer F H R Baraldi	86332	Joined Sqn 29 Sep 40. Survived War.
Pilot Officer A J Blayney	90538	Posted from Sqn Aug 40. Later awarded AFC & survived War.
Pilot Officer C G Chappell	40672	Joined Sqn 11 Oct 40. Survived War.
Pilot Officer D M Crook	90478	On Sqn Aug 40. Awarded DFC 1 Nov 40. Reported missing with 8 OTU on 13 Dec 44 when Spitfire EN662 crashed in an accident 8 miles SSE of Aberdeen.
Pilot Officer J Curchin	43296	On Sqn Aug 40. Awarded DFC 1 Nov 40. Reported missing over the Straits of Dover whilst commanding B Flight 4 Jun 41 when Spitfire P8204 probably collided with Messerschmitt Bf 109F-2, *wk nr* 6707 coded <3+− of Stab I/JG 53 flown by *Feldwebel* Heinrich Rühl
Pilot Officer J D Gardner	82181	Joined Sqn Aug 40. Posted away Sep 40. Survived Postwar.
Pilot Officer G N Gaunt	91230	On Sqn Aug 40. Killed in action with Sqn 15 Sep 40.
Pilot Officer S J Hill	77795	Joined Sqn 29 Sep 40. Killed in action with Sqn 18 Jun 41 when Spitfire W3211/PR-H was shot down by a Bf 109 5 miles west of Dover.
Pilot Officer C Keough	81620	Joined Sqn Aug 40. Posted 26 Sept 40. Killed in action 15 Feb 41 while with 71 Sqn when Hurricane V7606 crashed near Chapel St Leonards.
Pilot Officer A Mamedorf	81621	Joined Sqn Aug 40. Posted 26 Sep 40. Killed in accident while with 13 Sqn 8 Oct 41 when Hurricane Z3781 crashed near Ramsey, Isle of Man.
Pilot Officer R F G Miller	42419	On Sqn Aug 40. Killed in action while with Sqn 27 Sep 40.
Pilot Officer A K Ogilvie	42872	Joined Sqn 19 Aug 40. Awarded DFC. Shot down by Bf 109s of Jagdgeschwader 26 near St Omer & taken POW whilst still with Sqn on 4 Jul flying Spitfire X4664.
Pilot Officer Z Olenski	76617	Joined Sqn 6 Oct 40. Survived war.
Pilot Officer M E Staples	83242	On Sqn Aug 40. Wounded in action with Sqn 7 Oct 40. Killed in accident while with 604 Sqn 9 Nov 41 when Beaufighter T4638/NG-F crashed at Quarry Hill, Middle Wallop.
Pilot Officer E M Taylor		Joined Sqn Nov 40; posted to 152 Sqn 29 Dec 40.
Pilot Officer E G Titley	86334	Joined Sqn 29 Sep 40. Killed in flying accident while with 5 OTU 17 Jul 43 when Beaufort JM514 crashed at Ryefield, County Armagh.
Pilot Officer E Q Tobin	81622	Joined Aug 40. Posted 26 Sep 40. Killed in action while with 71 Sqn 7 Sep 41 when Spitfire W3801 was shot down near Boulogne.
Pilot Officer J Zurakowski	76715	Joined Sqn 6 Oct 40. Survived War.
Sergeant R J Boyd	126765	Joined Sqn 25 Nov 40. Later awarded DFM. Later commissioned. Killed in action on 6 Sep 43 20 miles south of Fecamp when Spitfire MB716 of 41 Sqn was shot down by Jagdgeschwader 2. Buried St Riquier Es Plains.
Sergeant G C Bennett	740558	Rejoined Sqn Nov 40 following recuperation for wounds received in action 31 May 40. Reported missing in action whilst with Sqn 29 Apr 41 when Spitfire P7669 was shot down over the Channel.
Sergeant A N Feary	742301	On Sqn Aug 40. Killed in action while with Sqn 7 Oct 40.

Sergeant G P Hickman	748272	Joined Sqn Dec 40. Shot down and taken POW while with 92 Sqn 20 Sep 41 in Spitfire W3179. Shot by Gestapo Dec 44.
Sergeant J A Hughes-Rees	745790	Joined Sqn 18 Sep 40. Later awarded DFM. Later commissioned. Died of polio at Tel El Kebir 30 Apr 43 whilst with 73 OTU.
Sergeant R T F Mercer	748316	Joined Sqn 29 Sep 40. Killed in action while with Sqn 9 May 41 when Spitfire P7305 crashed at St Margarets Bay, Kent.
Sergeant A G Palmer	741982	Joined Sqn 5 Dec 40. Awarded DFM. Reported missing while with Sqn when shot down off Le Touquet 21 Oct 41 whilst flying Spitfire AD136/PR-K.
Sergeant S T Rouse	134762?	Joined Sqn late 40. Later commissioned. Killed in action 14–15 Mar 45 near Lutzendorf, Germany flying Lancaster PA214 of 227 Sqn.
Sergeant J A Short	745244	Joined Sqn Nov 40; posted to 152 Sqn 21 Dec 40. Shot down and taken POW near Brest 24 Jul 41 whilst flying Spitfire P8512 of 152 Sqn.
Sergeant W H Walker		Joined Dec 40.

609 Squadron Air Combat Kills August—December 1940

Date	Pilot	Type	Details
8 Aug 40	Plt Off M J Appleby	Bf 110	Off Isle of Wight, 1230 hrs
	Plt Off J Curchin	Bf 110	Off Isle of Wight, 1230 hrs
	Sqn Ldr H S Darley	Bf 110	Off Isle of Wight, 1230 hrs
	Flt Lt J H G McArthur	Ju 87	Off Isle of Wight, 1230 hrs
	Flt Lt J H G McArthur	Ju 87	Off Isle of Wight, 1230 hrs
11 Aug 40	Plt Off N Le C Agazarian	Bf 110	15 miles south of Portland Bill, 1015 hrs
	Fg Off J C Dundas	Bf 110	Off Swanage, 1015 hrs
	Plt Off J D Bisdee	Bf 110	Off Swanage, 1015 hrs
	Flt Lt J H G McArthur	Bf 110	15 miles SSE of Swanage, 1015 hrs
12 Aug 40	Fg Off J C Dundas	Bf 110	East of the Isle of Wight, 1230 hrs
	Plt Off H McD Goodwin	Bf 110	East of the Isle of Wight, 1230 hrs
	Plt Off C N Overton	Bf 110	East of the Isle of Wight, 1230 hrs
	Fg Off D M Crook	Bf 109	East of the Isle of Wight, 1230 hrs
	Fg Off D M Crook	Bf 109	East of the Isle of Wight, 1230 hrs
	Sgt A N Feary	Bf 109	East of the Isle of Wight, 1230 hrs
	Plt Off M E Staples	Bf 110	East of the Isle of Wight, 1230 hrs
	Plt Off N Le C Agazarian	Bf 110	East of the Isle of Wight, 1230 hrs
13 Aug 40	Plt Off C N Overton	Ju 87	Lyme Bay, 1555 hrs
	Plt Off C N Overton	Ju 87	Lyme, Bay, 1555 hrs
	Fg Off J C Dundas	Ju 87	Lyme Bay, 1600 hrs
	Fg Off H McD Goodwin	Ju 87	5 miles west of Portland, 1600 hrs
	Fg Off H McD Goodwin	Ju 87	5 miles west of Portland, 1600 hrs
	Plt Off R F G Miller	Ju 87	5 miles west of Dorchester, 1600 hrs
	Flt Lt F J Howell	Ju 87	5 miles off Warmwell, 1600 hrs
	Fg Off T Nowierski	Bf 109	Off Weymouth, 1600 hrs. Bf 109E-1, black 9+– of 5/JG 53 crashed into Weymouth Bay, *Fw* Pfannschmidt POW.
	Fg Off D M Crook	Bf 109	Weymouth, 1600 hrs. Bf 109E-1, black 10 of 5/JG 53. Crashed into Poole Harbour, *Uffz* Hohenfeldt POW.
	Flt Lt F J Howell	Ju 87	Lyme Bay
	Plt Off M E Staples	Ju 87	Lyme Bay
	Sgt A N Feary	Ju 87	Lyme Bay, 1615 hrs

14 Aug 40	Fg Off J C Dundas	He 111	Romsey, 1700 hrs. He 111 P, wk nr 2898, G1+AA of Stab/KG 55 crashed East Dean, Hants. *Oberst* Stöckl (*Geschwader Kommodore*) & 2 killed, 2 POW.
	Sgt A N Feary	Ju 88	Near Middle Wallop
15 Aug 40	Flt Lt F J Howell	Ju 88	
	Fg Off A R Edge	Bf 110	Romsey, 1750 hrs. Possibly Bf 110C of Stab II/ZG 76. Crashed at Broadlands near Romsey, 1755 hrs. *Uffz* Rohrich & radio operator killed.
	Fg Off P Ostazewski	Bf 110	Isle of Wight. Bf 110C, M8+BP of 6/ZG 76. Crashed 1806 hrs at Ashey Down, Brading. *Fw* Birndorfer killed, radio operator wounded POW.
	Flt Lt J H G McArthur	Bf 110	NW of Southampton
	Flt Lt J H G McArthur	Bf 110	15 miles SSW of above kill
25 Aug 40	Plt Off N Le C Agazarian	Bf 110	NW of Poole Harbour, 1710 hrs. Bf 110C-4, 3M+KH of 1/ZG 2. Crashed at Priory Farm, East Holme, Dorset. *Uffz* Becker & radio operator POW.
	Plt Off G Gaunt		
	Flt Lt J H G McArthur	Bf 110	In between Warmwell & Poole, 1720 hrs. Possibly Bf 110C-4, wk nr 2728 of 8/ZG 76. Crashed at Symond's Farm, Buckland Ripers, Dorset. *Fw* Dahne & radio operator killed.
	Sqn Ldr H S Darley	Bf 110	2 miles off Warmwell, 1720 hrs
	Sq Ldr H S Darley	Bf 109	4 miles off Warmwell, 1720 hrs
	Plt Off J Curchin	Bf 109	5 miles off Portland, 1730 hrs
	Flt Lt F J Howell	Bf 110	Portsmouth/Bournemouth area
	Sgt A N Feary	Bf 110	Coombe Keynes 1745 hrs. Bf 110C-4 of 1/ZG 2. Crashed Creech Barrow, Wareham, *Oblt* Götz (*Staffel Kapitän*) & radio operator POW.
7 Sep 40	Plt Off J Curchin	Bf 109	Thames Estuary, 1740 hrs
	Fg Off T Nowierski	Do 17	
	Flt Lt J H G McArthur	Do 17	
	Fg Off J D Bisdee	Bf 110	SW of London, 1800 hrs
	Flt Lt F J Howell	Bf 110	London, 1800 hrs
	Plt Off A K Ogilvie	Bf 109	London, 1800 hrs
15 Sep 40	Plt Off A K Ogilvie	Do 17	East of London, 1215 hrs. Do 17 Z, wk nr 2361, F1+FH of 1/KG 76. Claimed by numerous RAF fighters and crashed at Victoria Station. *Oblt* Zehbe & 2 killed, 2 POW.
	Plt Off M J Appleby	Do 17	Belly landed near Dungeness, 1210 hrs. Do 17 Z, wk nr 2555 F1+FS of 8/KG 76. Crash-landed at Castle Farm, Shoreham, 1210 hrs. *Fw* Heitsch & 2 POW, one killed.
	Plt Off E Q Tobin		
	Plt Off J Curchin	Do 17	North of Hastings, 1530 hrs
	Plt Off N Le C Agazarian		
	Fg Off J C Dundas	Do 17	1210 hrs. See details for Plt Offs Appleby & Tobin above
	Fg Off J C Dundas	Do 17	1530 hrs
	Flt Lt F J Howell	Do 17	1530 hrs

24 Sep 40	Plt Off J Curchin	Bf 110	Off Isle of Wight, 1620 hrs
	Sgt A N Feary	Do 17	Brightstone Bay, 1620 hrs
	Plt Off M E Staples	Do 17	Off Isle of Wight, 1620 hrs
	Fg Off J C Dundas	Bf 109	Off Isle of Wight, 1620 hrs
25 Sep 40	Sgt J A Hughes Rees	Bf 110	Off Portishead Point, 1130 hrs
	Plt Off J Curchin	He 111	Force-landed near Swanage, 1130 hrs. He 111 H, wk nr 6305, G1+BH of 1/KG 55. Crash landed at Studland, *Hptm* Köthke & crew POW.
	Flt Lt J H G McArthur	Bf 110	Bournemouth
	Fg Off J C Dundas	Bf 110	Bournemouth
	Plt Off N Le C Agazarian	He 111	Into a house east of Poole Harbour. He 111 P, wk nr 2803 G1+LR of 7/KG 55. Crashed at Branksome Park, Poole, 1208 hrs. *Oblt* Scholz & crew killed.
	Plt Off J Curchin		
	Fg Off T Nowierski	He 111	West of Bournemouth
	Plt Off R F G Miller		
26 Sep 40	Plt Off N Le C Agazarian	Bf 109	Southampton, 1630 hrs
	Fg Off J C Dundas	Bf 109	Southampton, 1630 hrs
	Plt Off J Curchin	He 111	30 miles south of Southampton, 1630 hrs. Possibly He 111 H, wk nr 5314, G1+BL of 3/KG 55. *Oblt* Graf Schweinitz & 4 missing.
27 Sep 40	Fg Off D M Crook	Bf 110	60 miles south of Weymouth, 1145 hrs
	Fg Off J D Bisdee		
	Fg Off J C Dundas	Bf 110	Portland
	Plt Off N Le C Agazarian	Bf 109	25 miles south of Portland, 1200 hrs
	Plt Off R F G Miller	Bf 110	Collided with Bf 110C-4, wk nr 3297, 3U+FT of 9/ZG 26 which crashed at Dole Ash Farm, Piddletrenthide. *Gefr* Jackstedt POW, radio operator killed.
	Plt Off A K Ogilvie	Bf 110	Portland
30 Sep 40	Fg Off D M Crook	Bf 109	Off Swanage, 1130 hrs
	Fg Off D M Crook	Bf 109	Off Swanage, 1130 hrs
	Plt Off M J Appleby	Bf 109	Weymouth, 1130 hrs
	Fg Off T Nowierski	Bf 109	Sydling St Nicholas, 1715 hrs. Bf 109E-4, wk nr 4861 of 5/JG 2, crashed at Sydling St Nicholas, *Gefr* Dollinger killed.
7 Oct 40	Fg Off J D Bisdee	Bf 110	Cerne Abbas, 1550 hrs. Probably Ju 88 A-1, 8064, 9K+SN of 5/KG 51. Crashed near Sydling St Nicholas, *Oblt* Hey & crew POW.
	Sqn Ldr M L Robinson	Bf 110	North of Portland. Bf 110C-4, wk nr 3564, 3U+JT of 9/ZG 26. Crashed at Corfe Castle, *Gefr* Demmig POW, radio operator killed.
	Sqn Ldr M L Robinson	Bf 110	Long Bredy. Bf 110C-7, wk nr 3418, 3U+JP of 6/ZG 26. *Ofw* Herzog & radio operator killed.
	Flt Lt F J Howell	Bf 110	10 miles NW of Portland, 1600 hrs

	Fg Off J C Dundas	Bf 110	6 miles north of Warmwell, 1630 hrs. Probably Bf 110C-4, wk nr 3283, 3U+BT of 9/ZG 26. Crashed at Stoborough, Wareham. *Lt* Sidow & radio operator killed.
15 Oct 40	Fg Off J C Dundas	Bf 110	Christchurch Bay, 1240 hrs
	Plt Off N Le C Agazarian	Bf 109	Poole area, 1240 hrs
	Fg Off T Nowierski	Bf 109	Lymington, 1245 hrs. Bf 109E-1, wk nr 3279, white 10 of 4/JG 2. Crashed at Everton near Lymington, *Gefr* Pollach POW.
21 Oct 40	Fl Lt F J Howell	Ju 88	Milford of Sea, 1345 hrs. Ju 88A-5, wk nr 8116, 9K+BH of 1/KG 51. Crashed 1347 hrs, *Oblt* Fabian & crew killed. <u>100th kill.</u>
	Plt Off S J Hill		
28 Nov 40	Flt Lt J C Dundas	Bf 109	Off Isle of Wight, 1615 hrs. Bf 109E-4, wk nr 5344, <+ of Stab/JG 2. *Maj* Wick (*Geschwader Kommodore*) missing.
2 Dec 40	Fg Off T Nowierski	Bf 110	Off Thorney Island
	Fg Off N Le C Agazarian		

609 Squadron Losses – August–December 1940

Date	Ac & Serial	Code	Pilot	Fate	Details
8 Aug 40	Spitfire P9322		Plt Off M J Appleby	—	Damaged in combat with Bf 110 of V(Z)/LG 1 off Isle of Wight
	Spitfire R6979		Sqn Ldr H S Darley	—	Damaged in combat with Bf 110 of V(Z)/LG 1 off Isle of Wight
	Spitfire L1082		Plt Off C N Overton	—	Force-landed at Christchurch due to lack of oil pressure
10 Aug 40	Spitfire R6979		Plt Off E Q Tobin	—	Damaged propeller tips on take off from Hamble
11 Aug 40	Spitfire R6918	PR-D	Plt Off J C Dundas	—	Ac damaged in combat off Swanage, 1035 hrs
12 Aug 40	Spitfire K9841		Plt Off N Le C Agazarian	—	Ac damaged in combat off Swanage, 1238 hrs
	Spitfire K9997		Fg Off H McD Goodwin	—	Damaged in combat with Bf 110s off Isle of Wight, 1230 hrs
	Spitfire R6692		Fg Off J C Newbery	—	Damaged in combat with Ju 88 over Channel, 1250 hrs
	Spitfire N3024	PR-H	Plt Off D M Crook	—	Wings damaged during high speed combat manouevre
13 Aug 40	Spitfire R6690	PR-A	Plt Off J C Dundas	—	Damaged in combat over Channel, 1625 hrs
	Spitfire R6691	PR-J	Flt Lt F J Howell	—	Damaged in combat
14 Aug 40	Spitfire N3024	PR-H	Fg Off H McD Goodwin	+	Shot down into sea off Bournemouth, 1730 hrs
	Spitfire R6961		Plt Off J C Dundas	—	Damaged in combat with Ju 88 5 miles SW Warmwell, 1740 hrs
	Spitfire R6692		—	—	Destroyed in bombing raid on Middle Wallop
	Spitfire P9322		—	—	Destroyed in bombing raid on Middle Wallop
	Spitfire R6977	PR-N	—	—	Destroyed in bombing raid on Middle Wallop
15 Aug 40	Spitfire R6922		—	—	Damaged in bombing raid on Middle Wallop

16 Aug 40	Spitfire L1065	PR-E	Plt Off M J Appleby	—	Taxied into Spitfire K9997 during scramble; both aircraft damaged
18 Aug 40	Spitfire R6699	PR-L	Plt Off V C Keough	—	Taxied into Blenheim of 604 Sqn; both ac damaged
19 Aug 40	Spitfire L1008	PR-K	Plt Off E Q Tobin	—	Lost oil pressure during patrol; force-landed at Worthy Down but overshot and ended up in hedge; ac damaged
24 Aug 40	Spitfire L1082	PR-A	Plt Off A Mamedorf	—	Severely damaged in combat with enemy fighter over Ryde, 1650 hrs
	Spitfire X4104		Flt Lt F J Howell	—	Damaged in combat over Ryde, 1650 hrs
	Spitfire R6631		Fg Off T Nowierski	—	Damaged in combat over Ryde, 1650 hrs
25 Aug 40	Spitfire R6986		Fg Off P Ostaszewski	W	Badly damaged in combat with Bf 110 over Swanage, 1730 hrs
	Spitfire R6961		Plt Off D M Crook	—	Damaged in combat with Bf 110 over Swanage, 1730 hrs
30 Aug 40	Spitfire L1096		Plt Off R F G Miller	—	Forgot to wait for trolley accumulator to be disconnected during practice scramble, turned and damaged rudder
2 Sep 40	Spitfire R6769	PR-D	Fg Off J C Dundas	—	Hit bofors gun on landing at Middle Wallop and crash landed; ac written off
7 Sep 40	Spitfire N3280		Plt Off A K Ogilvie	—	Damaged in combat south of London, 1735 hrs
	Spitfire N3113		Plt Off J D Bisdee	—	Damaged in combat south of London, 1730 hrs
	Spitfire R6915		Plt Off N Le C Agazarian	—	Damaged in combat with He 111 south of London, 1800 hrs
15 Sep 40	Spitfire K9997		Plt Off E Q Tobin	—	Hit vehicle coming in to land at Middle Walop, 1230 hrs; aircraft crash-landed
	Spitfire R6690	PR-A	Plt Off G N Gaunt	+	Shot down in combat & crashed at Castle Hill Farm, Addington Village, Kent, 1230 hrs
	Spitfire R6922		Fg Off J C Dundas	—	Damaged in combat with Do 17 over Rye, 1510 hrs
16 Sep 40	Spitfire R6922		Flt Lt J H G McArthur	—	Pilot forgot to lower undercarriage when landing at Hamble

25 Sep 40	Spitfire L1008	Sgt J A Hughes-Rees	—	Crash-landed near Glastonbury due to engine trouble, 1200 hrs
	Spitfire N3280	Plt Off A K Ogilvie	—	Damaged in combat wth Bf 109 south of Bristol, 1200 hrs
	Spitfire R6691	Fg Off J C Newbery	Inj	Suffered distorted wings, shattered hood and collapsed seat in high speed manouevre. Pilot suffered internal injuries
	Spitfire R6699	Fg Off P Ostazewski	—	Suffered distorted wings and shattered hood during high speed manoeuvre
26 Sep 40	Spitfire N3288	Plt Off A K Ogilvie	—	Damaged in combat with He 111 over Christchurch, 1635 hrs
	Spitfire R6979	Sqn Ldr H S Darley	—	Damaged in combat over Christchurch, 1640 hrs
27 Sep 40	Spitfire X4107	Plt Off R F G Miller	+	Collided with Bf 110C-4, wk nr 3297 coded 3U+FT of 9/ZG 76 over Cheselbourne & crashed at Piddletrenthide, Dorset, 1145 hrs
	Spitfire X4234	Plt Off M E Staples	—	Damaged in combat over Poole, 1215 hrs
	Spitfire R6915 PR-O	Plt Off N Le C Agazarian	—	Damaged in combat over Poole, 1215 hrs
	Magister N3929	Sgt A N Feary	—	Landing accident at Weston Zoyland, ac damaged
30 Sep 40	Spitfire R6915 PR-O	Plt Off N Le C Agazarian	—	Damaged in combat with He 111 north of Warmwell, 1730 hrs, force-landed at Warmwell
	Spitfire N3113	Plt Off J D Bisdee	—	Damaged in combat, 1730 hrs
	Spitfire R6961	Fg Off T Nowierski	—	Damaged in combat, 1730 hrs
5 Oct 40	Spitfire N3223 PR-M	Fg Off T Nowierski	—	Abandoned over Salisbury Plain due to undercarriage problems & crashed at Chisenbury, Wilts 1815 hrs
7 Oct 40	Spitfire N3238	Sgt A N Feary	+	Shot down in combat with Bf 109. Pilot tried to return to Warmwell but baled out too low. Ac crashed at 1630 hrs at Watercombe Farm, Warmwell.
	Spitfire X4472	Flt Lt F J Howell	—	Crash-landed at Vale Farm, Sutton Waldron near Shaftesbury after combat with Bf 109 over Yeovil, 1630 hrs
	Spitfire N3231	Plt Off M E Staples	W	Shot down by Bf 109 over Yeovil; pilot baled out burned over Blandford Forum & ac crashed at Shillingstone, Dorset 1630 hrs

	Spitfire R6915	PR-O	Fg Off J C Dundas	W	Damaged in combat with Bf 110 over Dorchester, force-landed Warmwell at 1635 hrs
15 Oct 40	Spitfire X4539		Plt Off N Le C Agazarian	—	Damaged by Bf 109 over Southampton, 1240 hrs
27 Oct 40	Spitfire P9503		Plt Off P A Baillon	—	Shot down in combat with Ju 88 over Andover; pilot baled out & ac crashed at Upavon
8 Nov 40	Spitfire X4560	PR-H	Plt Off Z Olenski	—	Burst tyre on take off but hit a soft patch on landing and turned over; ac badly damaged
10 Nov 40	Spitfire X4586	PR-O	Fl Lt J C Dundas	—	Collided with X4539 taxiing for a scramble; ac damaged
	Spitfire X4539		Plt Off N Le C Agazarian	—	Collided with X4586 taxiing for a scramble; ac damaged
13 Nov 40	Spitfire X4165		Flt Lt J C Dundas	—	Hit filled in bomb crater and ac went on to its nose, writing off airscrew
14 Nov 40	Spitfire X4590	PR-F	Sgt J A Hughes-Rees	—	Hit trolley accumulator lowering flaps
28 Nov 40	Spitfire X4586	PR-O	Flt Lt J C Dundas DFC	M	Shot down by *Lt* Rudi Pflanz, Stab/JG 2, 2 miles SW of Isle of Wight, 1615 hrs
	Spitfire R6631		Plt Off P A Baillon	+	Shot down by *Major* Helmut Wick, Stab/JG 2, 1615 hrs. Body washed ashore 5 Jan 41 at Ste Martin de Varonville & buried at Ste Marcouf.
	Spitfire X4590	PR-F	Plt Off A K Ogilvie	—	Damaged in combat
	Spitfire X4165		Plt Off J Zurakowski	—	Damaged in combat
2 Dec 40	Spitfire X4588		Plt Off A K Ogilvie	—	Overshot on landing at Warmwell and hit fence; ac badly damaged
18 Dec 40	Spitfire N3270		Plt Off S J Hill	—	Hit trees low flying damaging starboard wing

1 Staffel/Jagdgeschwader 53 'Pik As' Pilots August–December 1940

Name	Number	Ac*	Details
Hauptmann Hans-Karl Mayer	67005/01	2/8	With Staffel Sep 39. *Staffelkapitän* to 1 Sep 40; awarded Knight's Cross posted as *Gruppenkommandeur* I/JG 53 5 Sep 40. Killed 17 Oct 40 flying Bf 109E-7, *werk nummer* 4138 coded <+ (?). Body washed ashore 27 Oct 40 at Littlestone & buried at Folkestone.
Oberleutnant Hans-Martin Ohly	67005/14	7	Joined Staffel Dec 39. Became *Staffelkapitän* 2 Sep 40. Posted to be *Staffelkapitän* 7/JG 3, 4 Aug 41. Survived war.
Leutnant Siegfried Fischer	67007/8	8	Joined Sep 40 from 3/JG 53. Reported missing 2 Dec 40.
Leutnant Udo Padior	67006/17		Joined Autumn 40. Killed in air raid at Kursk, 1100 hrs 2 Jun 42 as *Oberleutnant*, buried Kursk.
Leutnant Alfred Zeis	67005/3	3	Joined Jan 40. Shot down & taken POW 5 Oct 40.
Fähnrich/Leutnant Walter Zellot	67005/24		Joined Sep 40. Awarded Knight's Cross. Shot down by flak & killed 20 km east of Wertjatschy, Russia on 10 Sep 42 flying Bf 109G-2, *werk nummer* 13487, 10+ (black 1, white 0).
Fähnrich/Leutnant Wolfgang Hauffe	67011/37		Joined Sep 40. Killed in action 29 Oct 44 as *Staffelführer* of 8/JG 53 when Bf 109G-14, *werk nummer* 780836, red 8+− crashed NE of Serres/Wiernsheim.
Feldwebel/Leutnant Ernst-Albrecht Schultz		2	Joined Sep 39. Wounded 2 Jul 41 flying Bf 109F-2, *werk nummer* 6731 west of Tarnopol. Rejoined II/JG 53 early 42, became *Staffelkapitän* of 5/JG 53 15 Apr 42. Wounded in air attack on La Marsa, 7 Mar 43. Promoted to *Hauptmann* & became *Geschwaderadjutant* Apr 44 until the end of the war.
Oberfeldwebel Alfred Müller	67005/6	6	With Staffel Sep 39. Shot down & taken POW 15 Sep 40. Died of appendicitis 18 Jun 44.
Feldwebel Heinrich Bezner	67005/7	9?	With Staffel Sep 39. Killed 26 Aug 40.
Feldwebel Heinrich Höhnisch	67005/10	5	With Staffel late 39. Shot down & taken POW 9 Sep 40.
Feldwebel Herbert Tzschoppe	67005/9	4	Joined Oct 39. Shot down & taken POW 15 Sep 40.
Unteroffizier Alfred Baumer	67007/17		Not confirmed whether on Staffel in 1940 but transferred from 3/JG 53. Injured in accident 30 Jun 41 at Baranowicz flying Bf 109F-2, *werk nummer* 5499.

* This refers to the ac usually flown by this pilot

Unteroffizier Wolfgang Bubenzer	67005/27		Not confirmed whether on Staffel in 1940 but killed 22 May 41 when Bf 109F-1, *werk nummer* 5685 crashed at Boulogne.
Unteroffizier Willi Ghesla	67006/12	12	Transferred from 2/JG 53 Jun 40. Shot down & taken POW 5 Oct 40.
Unteroffizier Werner Karl	67005/19	14	Joined May 40. Shot down & taken POW 2 Sep 40.
Unteroffizier Heinrich Kopperschläger		11?	Joined Staffel mid-1950. Transferred to Erg/JG 53 post-Sep 40. Killed Fontenex near St Jean D'Angely on 15 Jan 41 flying Bf 109E-4, *werk nummer* 5111.
Unteroffizier Rudi Müller		9	Joined Oct 1940. Missing 11 Dec 40.
Unteroffizier Ludwig Reibel	67005/13		Joined Staffel early 1940. Killed as *Oberfeldwebel* 20 Dec 42 when Bf 109G-2, *werk nummer* 14503, white 5 was hit by flak and crashed at Souk El Khemis, North Africa.
Unteroffizier/Feldwebel Heinrich Rühl	67005/21	10	Joined Staffel mid-1940. Posted to *Stab* I/JG 53. Reported missing in action when he probably collided with Spitfire of Flt Lt J Curchin of 609 Sqn, 2030 hrs, 4 Jun 41 whilst flying Bf 109F-2, *werk nummer* 6707 coded black <3-+-.
Gefreiter Josef Bröker	67005/21	15	Joined mid-Aug 40. Shot down & taken POW 25 Aug 40.
Gefreiter Heinz Sieg	67005/29		Not confirmed whether on Staffel in 1940 but wounded 28 May 41 flying Bf 109F-2, *werk nummer* 5430 which crash-landed at Berck Sur Mer following combat probably with Spitfires of 611 Sqn. Killed in action with Mustangs as *Feldwebel* 23 Jun 44 near Targsorul, Rumania flying Bf 109G-6, *werk nummer* 163650, white 3.

1 Staffel/Jagdgeschwader 53 Air Combat Kills August–December 1940

Date	Pilot	Type	Details
12 Aug 40	*Hptm* Mayer	Hurricane	1200 hrs, in sea off Portsmouth/Isle of Wight
	Uffz Rühl	Hurricane	1220 hrs, in sea off Portsmouth/Isle of Wight
	Hptm Mayer	Hurricane	1225 hrs, in sea off Portsmouth/Isle of Wight; ac damaged in combat
	Uffz Kopperschläger	Spitfire	1225 hrs, Portsmouth/Isle of Wight
13 Aug 40	*Hptm* Mayer	Hurricane	1600 hrs, in sea west of Portland
	Uffz Rühl	Hurricane	1600 hrs, west of Portland
	Uffz Höhnisch	Hurricane	1600 hrs, in sea west of Portland; ac slightly damaged
	Uffz Höhnisch	Hurricane	1600 hrs, in sea west of Portland
15 Aug 40	*Hptm* Mayer	Hurricane	1745 hrs, Salisbury
18 Aug 40	*Hptm* Mayer	?	
	Hptm Mayer	?	
	Lt Schultz	?	
22 Aug 40	*Lt* Schultz	?	
	Uffz Kopperschläger	?	
24 Aug 40	*Hptm* Mayer	Hurricane	1640 hrs, south of Isle of Wight
	Lt Zeis	Spitfire	1640 hrs, east of Isle of Wight. Probably Spitfire N3239 of 234 Sqn; Plt Off J Zurakowski baled out uninjured 1655 hrs.
25 Aug 40	*Lt* Schultz	Hurricane	1726 hrs, W of Portland, just off the coast
	Lt Zeis	Hurricane	1728 hrs, S of Portland
	Uffz Tzschoppe	Hurricane	1729 hrs, Portland
	Hptm Mayer	Hurricane	1730 hrs, W of Portland, pilot baled out & ac crashed into the sea 500m from the shore. Possibly Hurricane V7407 of 17 Sqn, Flt Lt A W Bayne baled out unwounded off Portland at 1725 hrs.
	Oblt Ohly	Hurricane	1730 hrs, S of Portland
	Lt Schultz	Hurricane	1730 hrs, SW of Portland
	Uffz Tzschoppe	Hurricane	1732 hrs, Portland

26 Aug 40	*Lt* Zeis	Spitfire	1630 hrs, NE of Portsmouth
	Hptm Mayer	Hurricane	1630 hrs, E of Portsmouth
	Hptm Mayer	Spitfire	1635 hrs, Portsmouth. Probably Spitfire X4188 of 602 Sqn, shot down off Selsey Bill 1643 hrs; Sgt C Babbage baled out unwounded.
30 Aug 40	*Uffz* Ghesla	?	
	Lt Schultz	?	
	Lt Zeis	?	
31 Aug 40	*Lt* Zeis	?	
	Lt Zeis	?	
	Lt Schultz	?	
	Uffz Ghesla	?	
4 Sep 40	*Lt* Zeis	?	
	Lt Schultz	?	
7 Sep 40	*Lt* Schultz	?	
	Uffz Rühl	?	
	Uffz Ghesla	?	
	Uffz Kopperschläger	?	
8 Sep 40	*Lt* Zeis	?	
	Uffz Rühl	?	
9 Sep 40	*Lt* Schultz	Hurricane	1730 hrs, eastern outskirts of London
	Fw Tzschoppe	Hurricane	1735 hr, London
	Uffz Kopperschläger	Hurricane	
12 Sep 40	*Lt* Zeis	Blenheim	1615 hrs, Le Havre. Combat between 3 Blenheims of 235 Sqn escorting 3 Blenheims of 59 Sqn; no ac lost.
15 Sep 40	*Uffz* Ghesla	Spitfire	1200 hrs, SE of London. Believed to be Hurricane P3080 of 1 Sqn RCAF which crashed at 1204 hrs near Tunbridge Wells; Fg Off A D Nesbitt baled out wounded.
	Lt Schultz	Hurricane	1200 hrs
	Uffz Ghesla	Hurricane	12?? hrs
	Uffz Kopperschläger	Hurricane	1210 hrs. Possibly Hurricane P3876 of 1 Sqn RCAF which crashed at 1210 hrs near Staplehurst; Fg Off R Smither killed.
	Uffz Rühl	Spitfire	1450 hrs, S of London. Possibly Hurricane P3577 of 303 Sqn. Sgt M Brzezowski missing.
15 Sep 40	*Uffz* Kopperschläger	Spitfire	1450 hrs, London. Possibly Hurricane P3939 of 303 Sqn which crashed at Stoke, Isle of Grain, 1451 hrs; Sgt T Andruszkow baled out unwounded.

1 Staffel/Jagdgeschwader 53 'Pik As' Losses, August–December 1940

Date	Pilot	Fate	Ac	Details
12 Aug 40	*Hptm* Hans-Karl Mayer	Uninj	Bf 109E-4, white 8	Damaged in combat
13 Aug 40	*Uffz* Heinrich Höhnisch	Uninj	Bf 109E-4, *wk nr* 1508, white 5	Damaged in combat
18 Aug 40	*Oblt* Hans Ohly	Uninj	Bf 109E-4, white 7	Engine malfuncton & force-landed at Montbourg, 1205 hrs
	Oblt Hans Ohly	Uning	Bf 109E-4, white 7	Undercarriage malfunction & returned to Cherbourg-East, 1745 hrs
19 Aug 40	*Oblt* Hans Ohly	Uninj	Bf 109E-4, white 7	Undercarriage malfunction & landed at Rennes, 1125 hrs
20 Aug 40	*Uffz* Willi Ghesla	Uninj	Bf 109E-1	Landing accident, Rennes, 35% damage
25 Aug 40	*Gefr* Josef Bröker	Wounded POW	Bf 109E-1, white 15	Shot down during escort mission by Plt Off Beaumont, 152 Sqn, Plt Off Beamont, 87 Sqn & Sgt Llewellyn, 213 Sqn; crash-landed at Tatton House Farm, Buckland Ripers, Dorset, 1730–1740 hrs
26 Aug 40	*Fw* Heinrich Bezner	Killed	Bf 109E-4	Crashed off Portsmouth due to engine failure during *Freie Jagd* 1550–1710 hrs. Body washed ashore at Boulogne 22 Sep 40
2 Sep 40	*Uffz* Werner Karl	Slightly wounded POW	Bf 109E-1, *wk nr* 3584, white 14	Damaged during escort mission probably by Fg Off Trueman of 253 Sqn & shot down by Sgt Lacey of 501 Sqn; crash-landed at Hythe, 0817 hrs
	Uffz Heinrich Rühl	Slightly injured	Bf 109E-4, *wk nr* 1569, white 10?	Crashed into Channel off Dover during escort mission. Pilot rescued.

9 Sep 40	*Fw* Heinrich Höhnisch	Burned POW	Bf 109E-4, *wk nr* 1508, white 5	Shot down during escort mission; pilot baled out & landed at Tatsfield; ac crashed at Cherry Lodge Farm, Old Jail Lane, Biggin Hill, 1800 hrs
12 Sep 40	*Lt* Alfred Zeis	—	Bf 109E	Damaged in combat with Blenheims of 235 Sqn; landed at Octeville 1615 hrs
15 Sep 40	*Ofw* Alfred Müller	POW	Bf 109E-4, *wk nr* 1345, white 6	Shot down during escort mission; believed ditched in Channel
	Fw Herbert Tzschoppe	Burned	Bf 109E-4, *wk nr* 5197, <+	Shot down during escort mission by Plt Off Lovell, 41 Sqn; pilot baled out & ac crashed at Addisham Court, Canterbury, 1210 hrs
	Not known	Uninj	Bf 109E-4, *wk nr* 5111	Landed damaged at Etaples after combat
25 Sep 40	*Oblt* Hans Ohly	Uninj	Bf 109E-4, white 7	Engine failure during combat mission and landed at Etaples, 0845 hrs
5 Oct 40	*Lt* Alfred Zeis	POW	Bf 109E-4, *wk nr* 1564, white 3	Probably shot down during escort mission by 1 Sqn RCAF or 303 Sqn; pilot baled out & ac crashed at Pluckley, 1145 hrs
	Uffz Willi Ghesla	Slightly injured POW	Bf 109E-4, *wk nr* 1804, white 10	Probably shot down during escort mission by 1 Sqn RCAF; crash-landed between Frith Farm Aldington & New Barn Farm, Bilsington, 1145 hrs
28 Oct 40	Not known	Uninj	Bf 109E-8, *wk nr* 6395	Crashed at Boulogne; ac written off
17 Nov 40	*Fhr* Wolfgang Hauffe	Uninj	Bf 109E-4, *wk nr* 5076	Crash-landed Etaples, 45 % damage
2 Dec 40	*Lt* Siegfried Fischer	Missing	Bf 109E-4, *wk nr* 5328, white 8	Missing from *Freie Jagd* off Dungeness, 1230 hrs after combat with Spitfires of 74 Sqn. Shot down by Sqn Ldr Malan off Dungeness 1224 hrs
	Fhr Wolfgang Hauffe	Wounded	Bf 109E-4, *wk nr* 1350	Crashed into Channel at 1240 hrs after combat with Sgt Glendinning & Sgt Morrison of 74 Sqn. Pilot rescued
11 Dec 40	*Uffz* Rudi Müller	Missing	Bf 109E-8, *wk nr* 4882, white 9	Crashed into Channel, probably due to icing